Towards the Light

A PORTRAIT OF WITHINGTON GIRLS' SCHOOL

Towards the Light

A PORTRAIT OF WITHINGTON GIRLS' SCHOOL

THIRD MILLENNIUM
PUBLISHING, LONDON

CONTENTS

Foreword – Sue Marks 6
Commemoration of the Founders – Elisabeth Lee 8
Introduction 10

PART ONE: HISTORY

Chapter One – 1890–1940: Origins and Originality 14
   Anthony Burton and Monica Hastings
Chapter Two – 1940–1990: Challenges and Opportunities 28
   Anthony Burton and Monica Hastings
Chapter Three – 1990–2015: Change and Constancy 44
   Sarah Haslam

PART TWO: SCHOOL LIFE

Chapter Four – The School Community 58
   Christine Davies
Chapter Five – Academic Life 70
   Ian Mckenna
Chapter Six – Creative Life 82
   Music – Gilly Sargent 82
   Drama – Jen Baylis 92
   Art – Ruth Fildes 98
Chapter Seven – Sporting Life 104
   Mary Rawsthorn

PART THREE: THE WORK OF LIFE

Chapter Eight – Outside the Classroom	116
Nadine West	
Chapter Nine – Manchester and the Local Community	126
Janet Pickering	
Chapter Ten – Withington and the Wider World	134
Julie Buckley	

About the Authors	146
Governance and Chairs of the Governing Body of Withington Girls' School	150
Headmistresses of Withington Girls' School	151
Forms and Years	152
Resources	153
List of Subscribers	154
Index	157
Acknowledgements and Thanks	159

FOREWORD

Sue Marks, Headmistress 2010–

As we anticipate the 125th anniversary of the foundation of Withington Girls' School, I feel immensely privileged to be the tenth Headmistress in its remarkable history. The Founders, when they met in 1889 at Lady Barn House, Withington, to discuss the possibility of establishing a "continuation school" for their daughters, could scarcely have imagined that the resultant school would prosper and develop to attain national recognition as a centre of excellence in school education. From its first four pupils in 1890, the School has developed to the current total of around 640 – large enough to offer a challenging and contemporary range of academic subjects and extra-curricular activities, yet still sufficiently small that every girl is known as an individual.

Excellent schools never stop striving for "incremental improvement" and, as this commemorative book was going to press, the School announced the exciting news of the intended construction of a purpose-built new Junior School behind the Arts Centre. The new building is planned for completion in time to mark the 125th anniversary in 2015, along with the planned enclosure of the resultant courtyard to create a light, bright, functional internal "hub" space beneath the Arts Centre for circulation, recreation and displays of girls' work.

The ethos, aims and values of the Founders have influenced the development of the School from its inception, and they continue to provide the framework for current procedures and plans for the future. The Founders' vision – remarkable in its time – was to prepare girls for higher education and "the work of life". It prescribed greater emphasis than was then usual in girls' schools on science as a training in observation and reasoning, on "manual training" and on outdoor games. The Founders expected that schoolwork should be its own reward, rather than relying on examinations and prizes "as motives for exertion". These tenets continue to underpin Withington's development in the 21st century, although we naturally take great pleasure in our girls' success in public examinations and national competitions. From our foundation, it has remained the aim of successive Headmistresses and Governing Bodies that the fees charged should be "as moderate as is consistent with the efficiency of the School", and the bursaries offered by the WGS Trust today make it possible for many girls to attend the School irrespective of their families' financial circumstances. I believe the Founders would approve wholeheartedly of the opportunities the Bursary programme offers to girls from the Manchester area.

Withington's Senior Leadership Team in 2014. Left to right: Ian Mckenna, Kathryn Burrows, Sue Marks, Sharon Senn, Sarah Haslam.

This book is not a historical narrative in the accepted sense, but rather a compilation of personal impressions of, and responses to, the School past and present. With so very many distinguished current and former staff and pupils to choose from, it has unfortunately not been possible to include references to every individual we might have wished, and so we have sought to mention by name what might be considered a "representative sample" of those who have taught and studied at Withington over the years.

This book owes a great debt to the School's archives and to the history written in 1990 for the first hundred years by one of my predecessors, Miss Marjorie Hulme. I should like to express deep gratitude to her; to Marie Green, who wrote the Centenary publication *Withington Girls' School: A celebration of the first hundred years*; and to all those current and former staff and pupils who have contributed whole chapters, boxes, anecdotes, memories or photographs to this commemorative book. We have tried to include as much as possible. Thanks must also go to our Editor, Deborah Coleman, who has worked wonders in helping us all master the discipline of bringing what began as a tentative idea in 2012 to this end result – an affectionate insight into the history and present of this remarkable school.

Withington in the 21st century is a school with a strong sense of its unique heritage and a powerful vision for its future in an increasingly technological and globalised world. We who have the privilege of being the School's current custodians look to that future with confidence, striving to build on the efforts of those who have gone before us, and always looking to move onward and upward – *Ad Lucem*: Towards the Light.

COMMEMORATION OF THE FOUNDERS

Elisabeth Lee, Chair of the Governing Body

For me, one of the most important events of the school year falls on Founders' Day when by tradition the Chair of Governors reads aloud the Recital of the Founders. I value this opportunity to connect with our past, and to honour the women and men who founded our school and the part they played in the advancement of girls' education. I am proud that the spirit in which the School began is still so evident today and I consider it a privilege to help perpetuate it. In the words of the Recital:

"It is fitting that on this formal commemoration of Founders' Day we remember the name and example of Charles Prestwich Scott. Born in 1846, editor when 25 years old of the Manchester Guardian, *he was in 1890 one of the Founders of Withington Girls' School, retaining this office after he had resigned every other.*

Loving truth, duty and the exercise of reason, Charles Prestwich Scott and his wife Rachel wished for the school knowledge through difficulty rather than success through ease. In their company were to be found others, founders and benefactors who alike had pleasure in uprightness and who set their affection upon the foundation.

Of these are Adolphus William Ward, Principal of Owens College, Vice Chancellor of the University of Manchester, first Chairman of the Governors, wise in Humanity, eloquent in Literature; Henry Simon, first Treasurer, early Director of the School's practical affairs, which interest Emily Simon, his wife, long continued. Out of her forethought and generosity, Mrs Simon gave to the School its playing fields and further endowed in the University of Manchester an Entrance Scholarship for Withington girls.

Caroline Herford, first Secretary, in whose home the decision to found the School was taken; Louisa Lejeune, longest of the Foundation Governors to serve in office, uniting in her courageous personality those gifts of learning and virtue freely bestowed upon the School by all its Founders.

In the imagination of our thoughts we keep their name."

INTRODUCTION

For centuries, education was the privilege of the rich, while the poor did without. Among the rich, boys were much better served than girls. In England a turning point came in 1868 with the report of the Taunton Commission (the Schools Inquiry Commission), notable because it included a section on education for girls. It acknowledged the prevailing attitudes of the time:

> *Parents who have daughters will always look to their being provided for in marriage, will always believe that the gentler graces and winning qualities of character will be their best passports to marriage, and will always expect their husbands to take on themselves the intellectual toil and the active exertions needed for the support of the family.*

But the report powerfully argued that girls' education should be intellectually the equal of boys' education. It built upon the work already accomplished by the pioneers of women's education, such as Frances Mary Buss, Principal of the North London Collegiate School for girls from 1857 to 1894, Dorothea Beale, Principal of Cheltenham Ladies' College from 1856 to 1906, and Emily Davies, who founded Girton College, Cambridge in 1869. From the 1870s on there were great advances in education for girls, and one of the pioneers was Withington Girls' School, an experimental school in a Manchester suburb – now one of the country's leading girls' schools.

The Founders' Vision

PROPOSED HIGHER GIRLS' SCHOOL FOR WITHINGTON AND DISTRICT

October 1889

For some time past the need has been felt of a Girls' School in this District, which should give a thoroughly efficient education to girls who have passed the preparatory stage of instruction.

At a meeting held at Lady-Barn House, Fallowfield, on Wednesday, October 16th, Dr Ward in the Chair, it was resolved: "That it is desirable to establish a School in this neighbourhood for the education of girls not under twelve years of age;"

And the following Committee, with power to add to their number, were appointed to take steps for carrying out this object: Dr Ward, Mr H. Simon, Mrs Lejeune, Dr Adamson, Mr E.A. Parry, Mrs Simon, Mr C.P. Scott, Mrs Scott, Miss C. Herford.

The general aim of the School will be to develop the faculties, both intellectual and physical, of the pupils, so as to enable them to continue their own education after they have left school, and to prepare them for the work of life.

The endeavour will be to make the work of the School interesting and stimulating in itself, rather than to depend on examinations and prizes as motives to exertion.

In all the teaching, mastery of one step in a subject before the next is entered upon will be aimed at, and thoroughness will be treated as the first condition of real progress.

The importance of Natural Science as a training in accuracy of observation and reasoning, and as giving a hold on the realities of life, will be fully recognised in the school course.

More prominence will be given to Manual Training and Out-door Games than is usual in Girls' schools.

The School will be conducted by highly qualified teachers, under the management of a Committee, and the fees charged will be as moderate as is consistent with the efficiency of the School, the primary object of which will be the advancement of education rather than profit.

It is necessary that the School should be ultimately self-supporting, but the assistance of the public will be needed in order to meet the initial outlay, and to provide against loss during the first few years.

It is estimated that a sum of at least £1,000 will be needed, and for this the Committee appeal to those who regard the School as likely to be of public service.

Donations by way either of gift or of loan may be made through any Member of the Committee, or can be sent to – The Treasurer – H. SIMON, Esq., 20, Mount Street, Manchester; Or the Hon. Secretary – Miss C. HERFORD, Lady-Barn House, Fallowfield.

1 History

"And now the school is of age it can claim its inheritance, if not of gold and silver, of many noble and kindly memories and many encouraging and inspiring traditions. Let us trust that a future is before it which, while not unequal to its past, will refuse to forget those memories or to allow those traditions to become obscured."

– ADOLPHUS WARD, FOUNDER, 1911

Chapter One

1890–1940: ORIGINS AND ORIGINALITY

Anthony Burton and Monica Hastings

"The school is in several respects unlike any I have visited – it is extremely desirable that so useful an experiment should not hurriedly be given up."

— THE SCHOOL'S FIRST INSPECTOR, MR KITCHENER, 1893

Withington Girls' School was founded in 1890, by some of Manchester's most influential citizens, in a city with a new tradition of liberal thought and a belief in education.

The Founders' vision for the School set out a new approach to education for girls. Its principles still hold true today, 125 years later, and have helped shape Withington's special character and its acknowledged position as an exceptional school.

Nineteenth-century Manchester was largely a creation of the industrial revolution and a trade centre for cotton manufacturing. It was, after London, the acknowledged second city of England and, despite the dark underbelly of poverty and exploitation revealed in Friedrich Engels' *The Condition of the Working-Class in England* (1845), had a fine record in supporting culture. In 1852 it was amongst the first towns to establish a free public library, and its 1857 Art Treasures Exhibition was probably the biggest art exhibition that had ever been staged at that time. Learned societies, like the Royal Manchester Institution (1823) and the Athenaeum (1835), occupied distinguished buildings, and from 1858 Manchester was the home of the Hallé, the first symphony orchestra in Britain.

Above all, Manchester promoted higher education. A bequest from a local cotton merchant, John Owens (1790–1846), enabled the founding of Owens College in 1851 with fine buildings by Alfred Waterhouse. It was open to men only, albeit "without distinction of rank or condition in society", although women could attend lectures and classes held off site. Despite a London periodical's comments in 1877 that "anyone educated in Manchester would certainly be dull and probably vicious", the College attracted good scholars to teach academic courses. In 1884 it became a part of the Victoria University – open to women as well as men – which also had colleges in Liverpool and Leeds, and in 1903 achieved independence as Manchester University.

Owens College lay to the south of the city, along Oxford Road, where in later years a substantial university campus has developed. A little further south were the suburbs of Fallowfield,

---

Previous pages: Miss Grant, Headmistress 1908–1938, Miss Stansfeld, Head of the Bedford Physical Training College, and girls at the opening of the gymnasium, 1934. Opposite: Miss Grant, Headmistress 1908–1938, and pupils around 1915.

Above: A bird's-eye view of Manchester in 1889. Illustration for The Graphic, *9 November 1889. Opposite: top right: Madeline Scott painted by Ford Madox Brown; bottom left: C.P. Scott.*

Withington and Didsbury, where the Manchester intelligentsia – including Withington's founding families – preferred to live. This was where the School too would make its home.

Withington owes its origins to a co-educational preparatory school opened in 1873 in Wilmslow Road, Fallowfield, by William Henry Herford (1820–1908). Herford had grown up partly in Manchester before training for the Unitarian ministry in York. He was a graduate of London University, spent some years studying in Germany and taught in Switzerland. He championed the educational philosophy of Johann Heinrich Pestalozzi (1746–1827) and his follower Friedrich Froebel (1782–1852), who advocated that the mental development of small children should be encouraged through discovery, imagination and physical activity, rather than by rote learning.

Herford's progressive school soon moved to Lady Barn House in Mauldeth Road, Withington, and still exists today in Cheadle Hulme. Herford himself retired as headmaster in 1886, handing over to his daughter Caroline (1860–1945).

It was at Lady Barn House that Withington Girls' School was first mooted, at a meeting on 6th October 1889 "to consider the desirability of forming a continuation school for girls of twelve years and upwards". Of those present, six are still commemorated each year on Founders' Day: Caroline Herford, Charles Prestwich Scott, Adolphus Ward, Henry Simon, Emily Simon and Louisa Lejeune.

The founding families knew each other socially, had similar liberal views, and were in many ways ahead of their time. They were passionate advocates of education for women and wanted their daughters to have the same academic opportunities as boys had at public school. They intended the new school to continue the kind of progressive education begun at Lady Barn House, and to prepare its pupils for higher education. All C.P. Scott's children and 15 of his grandchildren attended Lady Barn; his daughter Madeline was one of the first four pupils at Withington, and her children and grandchildren followed her to the School. A.W. Ward's daughter Adelaide also attended WGS, as did the three daughters of Henry and Emily Simon, and the four academically high-flying daughters of Louisa Lejeune.

Eleven weeks after the first meeting, money had been raised, premises acquired and a Headmistress appointed. That a small group of parents could expeditiously effect this testifies to their influential positions in the Manchester community.

Best remembered nowadays is C.P. Scott (1846–1932). Scott was the legendary editor of the *Manchester Guardian* for 57 years (1872–1929) and subsequently its owner.

C.P. Scott

Charles Prestwich Scott took a keen interest in education. He was a trustee of Owens College, a member of its Council from 1890–1898, and Chair of the WGS Governors from its foundation in 1890 until his death in 1932.

Despite his onerous duties as the young editor of the *Manchester Guardian* and as Liberal MP for Leigh from 1895 to 1906, Scott kept a close and caring watch on progress at the School, supporting it financially with his own money on more than one occasion to prevent its accounts being overdrawn in the early years. He helped Headmistress Miss Grant with the minutiae of school business – from drains to inspections and formal ceremonies – and, in her own words, generally supported her in creating the ideal of a girls' school "with a sane and balanced outlook".

Scott and his wife Rachel, one of the first students at Girton College, Cambridge, were firm believers in the Women's Suffrage Movement. Rachel Scott also attended Withington Governors' meetings throughout her life, so important to them both was the cause of girls' education.

Their only daughter Madeline was painted on a tricycle around the age of ten by Ford Madox Brown when the artist was working at the Town Hall on his *Manchester Murals*, a celebration of the history of Manchester. Madeline was one of WGS's four original pupils and the education she received there led to her entering Somerville College, Oxford, to read English in 1899.

Scott "taught his *Guardian* public to trust his integrity, to rely on the facts he told them, to respect his judgement and to listen to his criticism" (*New Statesman*, January 1932). Respect for him was such that he received the Freedom of the City of Manchester in 1930. His funeral at Manchester Cathedral drew a huge congregation representing all aspects of Manchester life, including the Earl of Derby and the Lord Mayor of Manchester. The funeral cortege processed from the Cathedral to the Manchester Crematorium, pausing as it passed the *Guardian* offices, and proceeding via Oxford Street and Oxford Road, where crowds densely lined the pavements and stood, bareheaded, in silence. He was one of the great men of our time.

Lucille Holden and Val Hempstock

TOWARDS THE LIGHT: A PORTRAIT OF WITHINGTON GIRLS' SCHOOL

Founders' Day

Founders' Day has been one of the highlights of the Withington calendar since its inception by Headmistress Miss Bain in 1947 in its present format, not only as a way of remembering the School's Founders, but also as a celebration of school life.

Much has remained unchanged over the years, including the recital of the Founders, the Headmistress's report and the rousing rendition of the school song, "Gaudeamus". The occasion is invariably enriched by musical contributions from the choir and orchestra; earlier years featured a Verse Choir, and later years readings linked to the chosen theme. Anecdotally, this time has always given the girls the opportunity to count the organ pipes!

Speakers have varied – eminent Manchester notables, Heads of Oxbridge Colleges, people well known in their own fields – but always with a strong emphasis on opportunities and possibilities for women. The Head Girl of the day gives the vote of thanks to the Speaker on behalf of the School, and in 2009 Mrs Pickering invited her first Head Girl and deputies to return to speak at her final Founders' Day – nine years after their leaving. They were inspiring role models for the younger girls.

One of the remarkable features of Withington is that no prizes are awarded for academic work, and Founders' Day provides the opportunity to congratulate all the girls in the Upper Sixth with the presentation by the Speaker of their chosen book. Much thought goes into the selection of books, and always there is some anxiety about the walk across the platform for the presentation, particularly in the Bridgewater Hall, where the distance seems so great!

Probably the greatest change over the years came when the venue moved from the Whitworth Hall to the Bridgewater Hall. Until 1999 the event was held in an afternoon at the University, with all the girls being transported down from School. The Whitworth Hall provided a remarkable and distinguished venue, emphasising the links between WGS and the University of Manchester. Unfortunately, it became impossible to fit everyone in after Health and Safety decreed that the organ lofts, which had for many years seated special guests, were "unsafe"! The Bridgewater Hall provided a spectacular alternative, with an evening ceremony, space for all parents who wished to attend, and the opportunity to include the older girls in the Junior School. Our first Founders' Day at the new location

Founders' Day. Opposite: at the Whitworth Hall in 1950 (top) and 1948 (below). This page: at the Bridgewater Hall in 1999, with Esther Rantzen presenting the leaving books.

Excitement mounted as we took our early lunch ... then it was all aboard the double-deck buses and off to the Whitworth Hall. Over the years Miss McCardell wore an impressive array of hats, one year bearing a resemblance to a Viking helmet - a formidable sight as she fixed us with a gaze to deter talking and fidgeting!

– CATHERINE WILSON (MEREDITH) (1962)

Miss McCardell stood, regally magnificent, until the whole school had entered, then raised her baton, paused significantly and tapped the music stand. We sprang to our feet, removed our blazers, rolled them up, put them under our chairs, and sat down again.

– MONICA HASTINGS (BURTON) (1964)

was the last of Mrs Kenyon's Headship. It was a great success despite nerve-racking preparations, including allocating every single seat in the auditorium and, for the musicians, mastering the great organ and the rising levels of the stage.

No memory of Founders' Day is complete without a mention of the rehearsals. These have become less elaborate and time-consuming, but for many years involved an afternoon when the old Sports Hall was filled with chairs and the whole school processed in, practising when to stand and sit, when to place coats under the seats and when to applaud. Skirt lengths were checked – in the 1960s to ensure that the then fashionable minis weren't too short and a decade later to check that the maxis weren't too long! "Gaudeamus" was sung, without crib sheets, until everyone was word perfect.

Dr Mary McDonald

Withington Girls School. June 1899.

Scott's paper gave regular accounts of life at, in his own words in 1924, the "pioneer enterprise" that was WGS.

Caroline Herford became the School's first Secretary and taught biology in its first year. An influential educationist in Manchester, she continued as Lady Barn's Head until 1924, when she moved south upon marriage.

Adolphus William Ward (1837–1924) was Principal of Owens College from 1889, and Vice-Chancellor of the Victoria University in 1886–1890 and 1894–1896. He had been Professor of both History and English Literature at Owens College, published prolifically in both fields, and went on to be Master of Peterhouse, Cambridge, and President of the British Academy. The first Chair of the WGS Council, he resigned because of doubts over the School's viability, but retained a close interest in its affairs.

Henry Simon (1835–1899) was a German-born engineer who founded a major engineering firm still in existence today. He and his wife Emily both served as school Treasurers, and often subsidised the School in its early, financially precarious, days.

Louisa Lejeune served as school Secretary for many years, and as a Governor until her death in 1936. Married to a Swiss cotton merchant who settled in Manchester, she habitually wore a "Liberty cloak of sage green, long and flowing, with a silver clasp and a sort of mushroom hat".

A printed circular proclaimed the Founders' vision for the School and its experimental nature: "the endeavour will be to make the work of the School interesting and stimulating in itself, rather than to depend on examinations and prizes as motives to exertion". It gave a prominence then unusual in girls' schools to manual training, outdoor games and natural sciences. In addition to the more traditional curriculum, subjects offered would go on to include sloyd (a type of woodwork originating in Sweden), nature studies and elementary astronomy.

The School was officially opened by the Lord Mayor of Manchester in April 1890. It had four pupils to begin with and a somewhat precarious early existence, reflecting its rapid

This page, L to R: Founders Caroline Herford, Adolphus Ward and Louisa Lejeune. Opposite: Emily and Henry Simon; the family grave at the Manchester Crematorium.

The Simon Family

Henry Simon arrived in England in 1860, aged 24. German by birth, he was also fluent in English and French. He had trained as an engineer in Zurich, specialising in the construction, functioning and theoretical base of machines. He founded two businesses, Henry Simon Ltd and Simon Carves, and his "Simon System" revolutionised flour milling across the world.

At Owens College (the future Manchester University), Simon founded a physics laboratory and established the chair of German literature. His support enabled the Hallé to continue after Charles Hallé's death; and he pioneered the building of the Manchester Crematorium, the first outside London.

After his first wife's early death Simon married Emily Stoehr, who bore seven of his eight children. The children attended Lady Barn House, the boys going on to Rugby. The Simons supported the founding of Withington, for girls including their daughters, by giving an interest-free loan of £1,000 to purchase the house on Mauldeth Road, where the School began.

After Henry Simon's death in 1899, Emily Simon succeeded him as Treasurer of WGS. She continued to serve as a Founder Governor and to support the School, by now at Wellington Road, financially. She is particularly remembered for her foresight in buying up the land around WGS before private building could encroach, so that it would have its acres of playing fields. She also endowed the annual Emily Simon Scholarship at Manchester University for a Withington girl going on to study there.

The Simons' daughter-in-law, Shena Simon, continued as a Governor until the 1960s.

Diane Whitehead and Val Hempstock

creation by a small group of supporters. Like other similar schools, WGS offered shares to local residents, but raised only £381 of the £1,000 hoped for. It was fortunate that the Scotts and the Simons were in a position to make repeated loans to keep the School going until it eventually became financially self-sufficient.

The key to financial success lay in balancing income from the fees paid by pupils with expenditure on staff and premises. Day girls paid eight guineas per term, weekly boarders 20 guineas, and full boarders 25 guineas. There was a maximum of 20 pupils during the first two years, rising to 25 by 1895 and 43 by 1902. Numbers peaked with 72 pupils in 1903 – benefiting from the closure of a nearby school – but fell back again to 51 in 1909. Some extra money was raised from services such as milk and dinner, which cost three guineas a term (the dry bread free to everyone went unreviewed, but the syrup tart and rice pudding drew praise). Charges were also levied for some types of tuition, such as dancing, drawing and sloyd. The School saw a small profit in 1897, 1898 and 1899.

Despite the range of subjects, the permanent staff was necessarily small: a Headmistress, one or two full-time assistants and some part-timers. From the first, WGS recruited teachers with the highest possible academic qualifications and relevant experience. The first Headmistress, Miss Margaret Ker, was a mathematician from Girton College, Cambridge, who had taught at Croydon High School. She appears however not to have given satisfaction, and was persuaded to resign in July 1891.

Her successor was Miss Margaret I. Gardiner, with a degree in natural sciences from Newnham College, Cambridge, and teaching experience at St Leonard's School, St Andrews. She introduced the first piece of WGS school uniform: a maroon velvet cap with the *Ad Lucem* crest. Abashed by the problems facing the School, she resigned in May 1896 when a timely legacy enabled her to start a school of her own.

In her place came Miss Alice Greenwood. Her father had been Vice-Chancellor of the Victoria University, and her family lived in Fallowfield. Schooled at Cheltenham Ladies' College, she took a first class degree in history at Somerville Hall, Oxford.

Her assistants included Miss Alice Ashworth, a graduate in English from Royal Holloway College, London with some mathematics qualifications; Miss Julia Marett, who had read classics at Somerville; and Miss Stella Leach, who had a degree in physics from Royal Holloway. Miss Greenwood, described as "a splendid and powerful woman", left in 1901 to pursue other academic avocations and Miss Ashworth stepped up to take her place. Although well regarded, she seems to have lost momentum after an initial burst of energy which saw the School move into new premises, and left to become Headmistress of St Albans High School in 1908. After this quick turnover of staff, the next Headmistress was to stay for thirty years, and it was under her guidance that the School stabilised and expanded.

CHAPTER ONE • 1890–1940: ORIGINS AND ORIGINALITY

It was my first visit to the school. It was quite a rural setting – I remember the beauty of a summer evening and the cheerful voices of the girls. The boarders were having a game on the field. I took Billy, my pet goat, with me and presented him, demure and well-groomed, to Miss Ashworth. I had the impression of very tall, active – slightly overwhelmingly active – people.

– EVELYNE SCOTT, A PUPIL IN THE 1890s,
LOOKING BACK 60 YEARS LATER

The qualifications of the School's teachers testify to its aim of achieving a high and varied academic standard. Its premises also reflected its growing ambitions. WGS started out in a leased house at 16 Mauldeth Road, with accommodation for staff, boarders and domestic staff, as well as two classrooms. It was not ideal: the roof leaked, fires smoked, strips of wood had to be inserted under the wainscoting to prevent draughts, and the drains smelled. Bailey, a local firm, were brought in to take care of the plumbing and proceeded to do so for the next 70 years. A playground was levelled and cindered, and, later, adjoining land was leased for a cricket field and tennis courts. By 1897, more space was needed, so the School leased Mosley Lodge, across the road, as teaching accommodation. The building at 16 Mauldeth Road became "The Boarding House".

By 1903 the School needed yet more space. Mrs Simon again came to the rescue, buying out a boys' school in nearby Wellington Road and leasing it to WGS. Woodlands had accommodation for staff and boarders, and "three excellent classrooms, a gymnasium, a laboratory and a sixth form room containing the library". It was still surrounded by farmland, some of which was leased for playing fields shared at first with grazing sheep.

WGS was to stay here and expand, its buildings gradually consuming the original Woodlands. In 1906, the School agreed it should buy the site, rather than lease it from Mrs Simon, but its financial affairs took some time to resolve. Nonetheless, the new accommodation promised a better future and scope for development, and in 1908 a new Headmistress arrived to mould this future: Miss Margaret A. Grant.

Above: Watching cricket at Mauldeth Road, around 1900. Left: the School at Wellington Road, 1903.

23

Miss Grant, appointed after an advertised open competition, had read history at St Hugh's College, Oxford, and taught English at Tunbridge Wells High School before coming to WGS. Taking over a somewhat precarious school, she faced numerous problems, and was sufficiently unsure of her ability to surmount them that she offered to resign in 1911. But she persevered; the School thrived; and pupil numbers grew from 55 in 1908 to 314 in 1933. The boarding house (which Miss Grant keenly supported) closed in 1919 owing to declining demand, and thereafter WGS was a day school.

An important early decision for Miss Grant and the Council concerned the relationship between the School, a private enterprise, and the developing state education system in England. The Balfour Education Act of 1902 had created a single new government ministry, the Board of Education, and given responsibility for education to Local Education Authorities (LEAs). LEAs were charged with creating new secondary schools (over 1,000 appeared by 1914, including 349 for girls), and were empowered, though not obliged, to support existing secondary schools and subsidise free places at them.

For WGS, co-operation with the Board of Education and the local LEA brought several advantages. The first was "recognition" of the School as efficient – which would increase its prestige and its appeal to parents. One of Miss Grant's first tasks was to prepare for the necessary process of inspection, and "recognition" was granted in August 1909.

Closer association with the state also offered the possibility of financial assistance, through the "free places" scheme or in other ways. Negotiations for "grant-aided" status were begun in 1917, though Miss Grant was reluctant to endanger her independence, and the School was placed on the Board's list of secondary schools recognised for grant from 1st August 1919. State money reached WGS principally through the free places scheme, whereby local girls, selected by the School through an entrance test, had their fees paid by the LEA. There were 22 free places in 1924, and 36 in 1933.

If the state was to give money, it required in return a stake in the governance of the School. Hitherto, the Council had consisted of the Foundation Governors, together with a varying number of co-opted members. From 1920, the Governing Body comprised eight representative Governors appointed by local authorities, one from Manchester University and one from the Senior Club (as the Alumnae association was then known), together with three Foundation Governors (Mr Scott, Miss Herford and Mrs Lejeune) and two co-opted members. It is recorded that Miss Grant "was accepted into the social and intellectual life enjoyed by the Founders, and she retained their friendship until they died, but their successors were

Above: Miss Grant, Headmistress 1908–1938. Right: Celebrating Founders' Day with games, 1925.

not all as congenial to her". Governors' meetings (one of her administrative assistants recalled) became more difficult: "what had previously been a rubber-stamp affair sometimes became a battleground where Miss Grant was on occasion worsted".

After C.P. Scott's death in 1932, Dr Edward Fiddes, a member since 1914, became Chair of Council until his own death in 1942. Fiddes had been Registrar of the University of Manchester, as well as Senior Pro-Vice-Chancellor and Ward Professor of American History. A link with the Founders was maintained through the daughter-in-law of Henry and Emily Simon. Shena, Lady Simon of Wythenshawe, was active in women's issues and Labour politics, and a member of Council from 1924 to 1967.

A further consequence of Withington's new grant-aided status was that it could no longer occupy rented property. In 1919 it took out a mortgage (paid off in 1929) to purchase the buildings it leased from Emily Simon. Mrs Simon died in 1920, and it transpired that she had crowned her generous endeavours for the School by bequeathing extra land for playing fields.

The Board of Education inspectors in 1908, considering all aspects of the School, praised its corporate spirit and the relationship between staff and pupils. They did however make some criticisms of the premises, especially the laboratory, and after further criticism new laboratories for chemistry and physics were completed by 1932. The buildings were much expanded during Miss Grant's time, but in piecemeal fashion, as funds became available. They were therefore rather incoherent, with various rooms opening out of each other, and abrupt changes of level. An early block of classrooms on the ground floor supported a gymnasium above: not a peaceful arrangement. A new gym was built in 1933 and the old one renovated as a library, and in 1930 a school hall was added.

The opening of the new gymnasium, 1934.

Miss Grant lived on the premises throughout her 30-year tenure, as did the Secretary, the lady gardener and four of the domestic staff. Electricity was installed in 1923. Miss Grant drove a car, so a garage was provided, but as she never learned how to reverse, the garage had doors at both ends.

The periodic Board of Education inspections also took curriculum into account. The Council had from the start commissioned independent inspections which were, on the whole, favourable, commenting amongst other things on the School's free and happy atmosphere and the individual attention paid to each girl. The later Board inspections had more bite, because on them depended the state grants. The curriculum had to conform to the state's expectations; the 1914 inspection noted that it was "based on the model of a first grade High School and included the various subjects proper to an extended Secondary School education for girls".

When a girl needed reproving, Miss Grant used to walk round the garden in front of the school quoting poetry to them.

– RUBY FRYE (McCAIG) (1939)

Dance display, mid 1920s.

A more structured curriculum led to more examinations. The Founders had not approved of exams, and the Inspection of 1908 still "found it satisfactory that the work was not hampered by the requirements of external examinations". The School's own academic standards were nonetheless high enough from the first for some pupils to take examinations in order to obtain recognised qualifications. Girls won open scholarships to Oxford and Cambridge, and embarked on medical careers, in what were still the earliest days of women's higher education.

As more and more girls reached the Sixth Form, and aspired to go to university, it became more and more necessary for them to pass examinations to satisfy the universities' matriculation requirements. In 1918 the state system established its own examinations, the School Certificate (taken at age 16) and the Higher School Certificate (taken at age 18), and by 1924 the WGS curriculum was geared to these examinations.

If the School was at first casual about examinations, it was equally so about record-keeping. Miss Ashworth had recorded the height and weight of each girl at the beginning of every term, but had not bothered to keep an admissions register or record where school-leavers went. Early inspections noted a similar "lack of restraint" in curricular arrangements, accuracy and discipline. Miss Grant was to address the former issues, but preferred to encourage self-discipline in her pupils rather than impose strict rules.

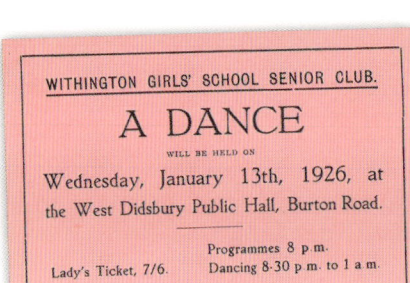

By 1914, inspectors had concluded that Withington "may be recommended with confidence to parents desiring a good High School education for their girls". In 1924, they found work in all subjects "satisfactory and in some excellent … the general atmosphere and spirit of the school is delightful". The experimental school was a proven success.

The Founders had stressed the importance of physical exercise. From the first, an hour was devoted each morning to games, with folk dancing in wet weather. This arrangement was still in force (except for senior Forms) in 1933, the Games Mistress being assisted by four visiting colleagues and other members of staff. "Games largely accounted for the freshness and vitality of the pupils," noted the 1924 Inspection.

During Miss Grant's time, fundraising was chiefly effected through an annual Arts and Crafts Fair. Her assistant, Betty Besso, recalled: "it was the high spot of the year and most of the autumn term was spent in preparation and anticipation". Art and craft was cherished in the curriculum, but Miss Grant was not so supportive of music, and discouraged girls from taking it up as a career. She was keen on drama, however, and kept up a vigorous programme, inaugurated by the Senior Club. A highlight was a 1912 performance – the first since the 17th century – of a Jacobean masque, *The Sun's Darling*.

At first, WGS served a small neighbourhood in south Manchester – the Simons' youngest child, Dorothea, came to school in a dog-cart from nearby Didsbury – but as its prestige grew it attracted pupils from a wider catchment area. By 1908, while most girls were from Manchester, three came from Marple, Stockport and Bolton. By 1914, there were more girls from Cheshire, perhaps because a new railway line had opened from Wilmslow. The 1924 Inspection noted that "comparatively few of the pupils come to school by train but the large number who cycle daily to and fro have the use of a frequent train service in inclement weather". C.P. Scott's granddaughter, a pupil at the School, recalled girls cycling home together "to and fro in Withington and Didsbury, lingering on the corner of the village by the White Lion, then slowly along Wilmslow Road, ever talking, and in the end parting reluctantly as though never to see each other again, although each knew the morrow would find her at W.G.S.".

In early days, there was a swift turnover of pupils: around 1914 over 30 per cent left each year. Ten years later, the average length of time that girls spent at the School was as little as two years nine months, but the school population gradually stabilised.

The 1914–1918 war did not interrupt teaching at the School, but casualties were so great that almost all families were touched in some way. Three of the Simons' four sons were killed in the war. They turned their home, Lawnhurst, into a military hospital, while girls raised money for those injured and knitted for those at the front. A number of pupils with German names anglicised them, and Latin replaced German in the curriculum.

As often with schools, the personality of the Head was of paramount importance. Reflecting Withington's own personality, Miss Grant was both scholarly and unorthodox. One of her successors noted that "for at least twenty-five years after she left and without any interference on her part, the rightness of any decision in school was judged by whether it would have met with her approval". She encouraged pupils to be intellectually adventurous, and tried to stimulate them – amongst other devices, introducing a new word at almost every assembly in order to expand their vocabulary. She conversed with the youngest pupils as one adult to another. But she had her more mischievous side. "She could fascinate when she chose and at other times could be really naughty and at times impossible," recalled Betty Besso. "She had a high sense of justice combined with liberal principles and yet was capable of strong and totally unreasonable prejudices; she was unrivalled in her handling of children and had always a certain indulgence for the sinner, provided the sinner had enough daring and style."

Miss Grant retired in 1938. Her successor was Miss Mary Elsie (known as Elspeth) Bain. A graduate in English from Edinburgh University, Miss Bain had been Second Mistress and Senior English Mistress at Sale High School for Girls, and the first Headmistress of Rochdale High School for Girls, a new municipal school. At Withington, she soon had to face the challenges and uncertainties of the Second World War.

Miss Bain, Headmistress 1938–1961, and pupils, 1939.

Chapter Two

1940–1990: CHALLENGES AND OPPORTUNITIES

Anthony Burton and Monica Hastings

"Our girls see no barriers, accept no limitations to their choice of course and career; and it is schools such as Withington which have helped to bring about this fundamental and irreversible change."

– MRS MARGARET KENYON'S CENTENARY ANNUAL REPORT, 19 OCTOBER 1990

In 1940, Withington celebrated its 50th birthday. But, in a Britain at war, celebrations were muted; and the occasion went unmarked until the Gold and Diamond Jubilees were commemorated jointly in 1950.

At the outbreak of war in 1939, plans had been immediately implemented for most of the girls to be evacuated to Uttoxeter, where they lived with local families. Their education continued at a local school, run on a shift system to fit them in. One pupil was billeted on a farm: "It was Heaven – I learnt to hand-milk cows, feed them, carry water to each animal in the winter, turn out and call them in … School was just a necessary nuisance between working with the cows."

Other girls were sent to live in America, or in safer parts of the UK, but some remained in Manchester, so the School continued to operate on the Withington site as well. Here blast walls and air-raid shelters were erected, and gradually pupils returned from Uttoxeter. The School escaped serious damage: although over 70 incendiary bombs fell on the grounds in Spring 1941, only one penetrated the buildings, and the flames were put out by Governors and staff on fire duty. The uncertainties of the wartime period did, however, cause a decrease in pupil numbers. Headmistress Miss Bain met the challenges with calm authority and cheerful confidence.

A major post-war issue for Miss Bain and the Council was the relationship of WGS with the state system. The wartime coalition government had introduced changes through the Education Act of 1944, heavily influenced by the 1938 Spens Committee Report (Shena Simon, a Withington Governor and daughter-in-law of Henry and Emily Simon, was a member of the Committee). The ideas in the Spens Report are not regarded highly nowadays. It stressed "the need in a highly industrialised

Opposite: Founders' Day at the Whitworth Hall, 1950.

War Memories

I am one of the boys who attended WGS after the South Manchester Grammar School Prep was bombed early in the war, and had four very happy years there under Miss Bain. Most of our lessons took place in our Form room at the corner of Wellington Road and Victoria Road, but we did venture out for assembly, PE in the gym and eurhythmics in the Hall, which the boys found rather funny, and I think we fooled around a bit. When we lined up for assembly in the morning we were each given a school hymn book. The boys thought it was great fun to tap each other's heads with the book when Miss Hardisty wasn't looking, but yours truly was caught doing this dastardly crime, and I was singled out every time we went to assembly by being given the oldest and tattiest book that could be found.

After two years in the prep we moved up to the main school. When we read aloud I was told (more than once) that I was the worst reader in the class, which did my confidence no good at all! I really enjoyed and listened intently to the Bible stories Miss Prouse told during her scripture lessons, so was surprised and bitterly disappointed when she did not give me a good report and said I was inattentive! Once or twice a week we did practical work, sometimes painting but usually raffia work. The girls were very good at this, but I struggled, particularly with bending the cane upwards to make the sides of my raffia basket. I soon decided that raffia work was not my forte! Arithmetic lessons were probably the best, and I am indebted to WGS for my ability even now to say all my tables as far as 12 12s are 144.

Geoffrey Barlow, 1941–1945 (pictured left)

society for post-primary schools of non-academic type with an orientation towards commerce or industry", and advocated a "tri-partite system" of schools: academic; "secondary modern", intended to equip children for the ordinary business of life; and technical, of which not many appeared. This only succeeded in buttressing the kind of "traditional academic course orientated towards the Universities" offered by WGS.

The 1944 Act established free compulsory education for all children between the ages of five and 15. Provision remained in the hands of the LEAs, now overseen by the Ministry (formerly Board) of Education and with considerably strengthened powers and responsibilities. The Act might have provided an opportunity for the state to establish control over church schools and independent schools, but in fact secured the position of both. Independent schools had to register with the Ministry, but, provided they did this, were free to go their own way.

Many, however, like WGS, had received financial support from the state. The Act provided for this to continue, but the terms of the bargain were changed. Previously, independent schools receiving government funding had been expected to reserve 25 per cent of their places for pupils paid for by LEAs, but WGS had initially secured agreement that it would offer ten per cent. After 1944, "direct grant" schools had to provide 25 per cent of places to children from state primary schools,

CHAPTER TWO • 1940–1990: CHALLENGES AND OPPORTUNITIES

Above: "As soon as we hear the wailing of the sirens everybody proceeds to get coats and gas masks" (a pupil, 1940).
Right: Clothes rationing lasted until 1949.

It was 1940, I was seven years old, and my earliest memories were the air raids, with the intrepid Misses Verity and Corfe fire watching on the roof, while everyone else crouched in the shelter and we little ones were distracted by a large tin of Mackintosh's Toffees (obtained from goodness knows where) as Miss Hardisty, our Preparatory Form Mistress, read to us from The Water Babies. *Extra clothing coupons were granted to children whose shoe size was a certain length. I never discovered the reason for this, but vividly recall standing barefoot in front of a line on the floor, and Miss Verity urging me to "spread your toes longer, Pamela". Needless to say the desired result was achieved. The end of the war brought relief from tension and a joyous service of deliverance in the Main Hall; but most necessities were still rationed, especially oil and coal, and a dreadful winter resulted in very little heating with girls wearing overcoats, scarves and mittens most of the day.*

– PAMELA BIRLEY (1950)

I arrived in 1940, a non-English speaker from Switzerland, and had to start several subjects from scratch. Miss Gearing was wonderful, she conveyed maths so clearly to me. I was older than the rest – when I caught up I could have jumped a class, but WGS was my sixth school in two years and I could not bear to lose my new friends.

– ANNA YATES (WIDMER) (1942)

Links with The Manchester Grammar School

Although there are few official affiliations between Withington Girls' School (WGS) and The Manchester Grammar School (for boys) (MGS), informal links are strong. Generations of sisters and brothers and parents and children; decades of joint academic and extra-curricular activities; professional and personal affiliations between staff and pupils - all combine to form an important bond between the two schools.

In the autumn term of 1940, Withington's Governing Council decided to admit 14 boys (along with eight girls) to a new Junior Department. The boys, some of whom Withington is still in touch with, came from the South Manchester Grammar School on Palatine Road, a preparatory school which closed on the outbreak of war. The new Withington boys were furnished with their own uniform, including a blazer and cap bearing the *Ad Lucem* crest, and enjoyed activities alongside the girls, forming the School's first "soccer" team. Some 36 boys attended Withington during the wartime period, the majority going on to MGS on Old Hall Lane at 11.

Records show WGS girls attending French plays at MGS from as early as 1912, and French and German topic lectures from the 1950s through to the 1980s. This paved the way for a successful joint French exchange programme with a counterpart Lycée in Paris in the 1990s. Withington's geography staff have invited MGS to join their pupils in Geographical Association competitions, while since the 1970s both classics departments have organised combined activities, including performances of plays by Plautus at MGS. WGS's classics department continues in this spirit, with a termly Latin Scrabble competition for GCSE pupils to help further their studies and enjoyment of the subject.

WGS and MGS staff have long collaborated on debates and lectures to encourage pupils' engagement in wider conversations. In the early 1960s, pupils from Withington, MGS, Manchester High School for Girls (MHSG) and William Hulme's Grammar School held a four-cornered debate, "That men are as clay and women make mugs of them" – oh to have been there. Dialogue between WGS and MGS pupils is still very much in evidence at meetings of PhilSoc and Junior PhilSoc, featuring a variety of talks on scientific themes by guest lecturers and researchers (see also Chapter 8). Model United Nations, also covered in Chapter 8, now provides another important platform for pupils to debate global issues. Delegations from the two schools travel throughout

Opposite: WGS staff, girls – and boys, early 1940s. Right: Singing in the Rain, a 2007 WGS and MGS co-production.

the UK to attend MUN conferences, including each other's.

WGS and MGS, together with William Hulme's Grammar School and Manchester Academy, comprise the "Four Schools Partnership", a programme designed to enrich pupils' mathematical experience outside the classroom. Each participating school organises four activities a year, recently including workshops at Manchester University, an open day at Oxford University and a mathematical tournament.

Drama and music have offered more opportunities to develop informal ties. Senior Withington pupils have taken regular performing and backstage roles in shared drama productions since the 1980s, benefiting from the extended performing arts facilities at MGS. Since the 1990s pupils from the two schools and MHSG have had the tremendous experience of working on drama productions and premieres at the Manchester Library Theatre, sometimes taking them on to the Edinburgh Fringe. Such productions include *I Magisti* and Alan Garner's *Holly from the Bongs*. Meanwhile GSCE and A-level drama students from WGS and MGS continue to put on productions together, notably *Singing in the Rain*, *Death on the Dial* and *Bed*.

Similarly there have been many shared musical performances. One initiative dates from the 1990s, when a small group of Senior School pupils at WGS, MHSG and MGS organised themselves informally into a four-part chamber choir, the Thursday Singers. The choir, conducted by a member of MGS staff, has evolved to include large numbers of Sixth Formers from the three schools.

Joint travels and charity work have also forged links. Pupils from the two schools have embarked together on numerous overseas trips, recent destinations including China and Uganda. And MGS Sixth Formers have been co-opted as models for Withington's now-famous Fashion Show. Organised by a committee of WGS Sixth Formers, the show raises several thousands of pounds for charity each year. MGS pupils take part in the fundraising too, and the result is a lively and fun evening for all involved.

With a host of joint curricular, extra-curricular and charitable activities to look forward to, the ties between the pupils of Manchester Grammar School and Withington Girls' School can only continue to strengthen and grow.

Clare Flynn

I lived a 25-minute bus journey away – made far more tolerable by the presence of MGS pupils. Some of us declined the school bus and walked to the bus stop on the main road to catch the MGS bus for the return journey (does this still happen I wonder?). I recall at least one pea-soup fog such that you could not see your hand if held at arm's length. The school bus could not run and we were let out of school early (hurray!).

– RUTH MORGAN (PIMLOTT) (1968)

At the resumption of peacetime life in 1945, Miss Bain recorded in the "Victory" *Newsletter* that there were 498 pupils at WGS, including 50 girls in the Sixth Forms. There were 29 members of staff, including five physical training mistresses. In 1950, Miss Bain noted that all the girls were "on the [playing] fields for some part of every fine day". So entrenched was physical education that her successor recalled that it was sometimes difficult to fit the rest of the curriculum around the many PE lessons. Miss Bain's efforts were mainly directed to improving "the general ability" of the pupils. She felt that the School had attained its maximum size, and further advance would lie in raising academic standards. When she retired in 1961, there were 531 girls taught by 27 full-time and two part-time members of staff.

The increased numbers of pupils, occasioned by direct grant status, put some strain on the buildings. So Miss Bain was almost continuously occupied with construction projects. In 1946 came a new biology lab, followed in 1950 by a housecraft room for needlework classes. In 1952 arose a new staff room and changing rooms for the gym. This project involved the demolition of "the cottage", a picturesque, timbered, one-storey building, which had been put up as a sanatorium in 1905, and later used as a staff room. In 1954, a new wing was erected to house four classrooms, a large lecture room and a domestic science room.

All these developments were very cautiously financed. Under the direct grant school regulations, schools were permitted to borrow to fund projects, but the Council, recalling the School's early debt-ridden years, refused to incur more debt, and only embarked on building when funds were in hand. However, in 1955 a group of major companies launched the

I was taking my French aural for School Certificate when there was suddenly a lot of commotion - Miss Bain running round the school shouting "Girls, girls, the war's over!" We got two days' holiday!

– MORAG MERICA (McCAIG) (1945)

and make available a further 25 per cent to LEAs if required. WGS chose to become a "direct grant" school, and the arrangement was advantageous: it channelled more pupils into the School, and paid for them, while still allowing the School to select them on academic merit. In the *Newsletter* for 1947, Miss Bain recorded that half the places in School were now freely available to girls supported by LEAs. Most came from the Manchester LEA area, but some came from Cheshire, Lancashire, Stockport and Salford.

CHAPTER TWO • 1940–1990: CHALLENGES AND OPPORTUNITIES

The school medical examination took place with Miss Corfe watching. She said my deportment was not good enough, and I had to report to the gym before Assembly to walk up and down with a book on my head! It did improve. We always loved the last gym lesson of the term when Miss Corfe announced we would play "Pirates", swinging on the ropes, climbing on the box, up the big frame, along the benches, all to get away from the imaginary pirates. When she blew the whistle, we had to be on the apparatus or we were out – a bit like musical chairs.

– VAL HEMPSTOCK (WINSTANLEY) (1956)

I suspect many schoolchildren have thought "Wouldn't it be great if our school caught fire!" It wasn't, even for the pupils, and it must have been a nightmare for the staff, especially senior management. The buildings smelled horrible and it felt strange to think an outsider had wanted to burn the school down.

– CATHERINE WILSON (MEREDITH) (1962)

Opposite: Miss Bain, Headmistress 1938–1961. This page, top to bottom: rear view of WGS in 1922, showing "the cottage"; the new domestic science room, 1954; the aftermath of the 1960 fire.

Industrial Fund for the Advancement of Scientific Education in Schools, to build and equip laboratories in independent and direct grant schools. WGS was awarded a grant on the strength of its science teaching, and a new science block opened in December 1957. Miss Bain's last building project was unexpected. Burglars broke into the School in June 1960 and set fire to the geography room and nearby rooms. Refurbishment enhanced these rooms, but there remained "an oddly shaped remnant never satisfactory for teaching purposes" (now part of the staff room).

TOWARDS THE LIGHT: A PORTRAIT OF WITHINGTON GIRLS' SCHOOL

Emily Verity MBE

Miss Emily Verity, known as EV, joined the staff in 1922 as a young physics graduate, initially teaching mathematics. Physics was soon introduced, and the quality of science teaching went from strength to strength. In the 1930s, Miss Verity designed the "old" chemistry and physics laboratories, and was in large part responsible for the grant from the Industrial Fund (awarded only to schools with high reputations in science) which enabled the lecture room and two other ground-floor laboratories to be built in 1957. Miss Verity retired in 1963, having been awarded the MBE for services to science teaching.

In wartime, her calm efficiency and concern helped the girls feel safe and confident, whether she was distributing sweets in the school air-raid shelters when there was an alert, or during the evacuation to Uttoxeter. Her sense of humour was apparent when the girls dammed a stream and consequently flooded the garden where they were billeted. Her only comment was "You should have known better – you put the dam in the wrong place!"

EV was an unusual and inspired teacher of physics, who cared for the non-scientific girls as much as for the very able. She had the girls running round benches as electric currents and chanting jingles to remember formulae: "acceleration down the plane is g sine alpha we exclaim!" She loved the School and maintained contact with many of her pupils through a multitude of letters until the end of her life.

Val Hempstock

Miss Verity once expressed regret to a class that so few streets in Manchester commemorated all its great scientists. Little did she know that the father of one of the pupils worked for the Manchester Highways Department. Not long afterwards, a new close in Withington was named Verity Close.

– CATHERINE WILSON (MEREDITH) (1962)

Miss Bain's good humour was rarely disturbed, but she sometimes felt under pressure from some members of staff who had served Miss Grant with devotion for many years. Miss Emily Verity had done more than anyone to develop physics teaching in the School, and Miss Ivy Corfe was in charge of physical education, clearly signalling her role by wearing a split

Staff in 1955. Some of those mentioned in this book are: top row, L to R: 3 Miss Hunter, 4 Miss Morris; middle row, L to R: 3 Miss Connell, 6 Mrs Rawsthorn, 8 Miss Boucher; bottom row, L to R: 2 Miss Finney, 3 Miss Corfe, 5 Miss Bain, 6 Miss Verity, 7 Mrs Hill, 8 Miss McCardell.

Miss Hulme, Headmistress 1961–1985.

skirt (or long shorts) to facilitate mobility. Highly cultured, she had a keen intelligence and a penchant for cold baths, and taught at the School for some 40 years. The deputy head, Miss E.M. Gearing, had a severity which could strike fear into the hearts of staff as well as pupils.

Miss Bain was Headmistress for 23 years. She ensured the School's survival through the Second World War, and her capacity to lead energised its expansion in the years of post-war reconstruction.

Miss Bain's successor was Miss Marjorie Hulme. Educated in Bury, she proceeded from the grammar school there to Girton College, where she read Mathematics and Moral Sciences (and was stroke in the Cambridge women's rowing eight). She had posts at the Collegiate School, Blackpool, and at Wade Deacon Grammar School, Widnes, before becoming Headmistress of Leigh Girls' Grammar School at the early age of 32. When Miss Hulme arrived at WGS (one of the pupils recalled), "we all noted the contrast between the slight, elegant figure of the new Headmistress and the imposing stature of Miss Bain. It very soon became apparent that the force of Miss Hulme's personality was not slight and she quickly stamped her character on the School." Miss Hulme was punctilious in discharging her obligations, and expected others to be the same, so her occasional lighter moments came as a surprise – as when the staff mounted a Christmas pantomime, and Miss Hulme appeared on stage as the Fairy Godmother in a midnight-blue tutu.

For some years, WGS's momentum under direct grant status continued, and Miss Hulme, like her predecessor, had to maintain a building programme to accommodate growing numbers of pupils. When she arrived, she found that the School had good specialist rooms, but not enough classrooms, and the kitchen and dining room were inadequate to feed the increasing number of hungry mouths. There were still, too, echoes of the war, with attics containing beds used by staff when fire watching.

Work on the new building project started in 1964. It brought six new classrooms and a new dining hall, constructed so that another floor could be added above it. This meant most of the original Woodlands building had to be demolished, and the sacrifice was reluctantly made.

It was clear that this project would cost more than the Council could hope to save, so, after much agonising, a loan of £24,000 was obtained from Manchester Corporation. For the first time since 1930 the School was in debt, but the loan was paid off within seven years. By 1970 plans were already afoot to construct a new library on top of the dining room, and this was soon achieved, the old library becoming a Sixth Form common room.

In the 1970s, the School once again faced a re-appraisal of its relationship with the state system of education. The

While the new dining room was being constructed Miss Brandrick organised soup for all in the main hall. We also brought sandwiches and became adept at stacking and unstacking chairs, organising dance sessions to the sound of the Beatles on wet days.

– MONICA HASTINGS (BURTON) (1964)

Top of the Pops was recorded weekly in Manchester during lunchtimes and the boldest two in our class used to bunk off unbeknown to staff, as well as to Liverpool to see the Beatles in the legendary Cavern.

– FRAN BARNARD (HOBSON) (1968)

"tri-partite" system of schools provided for by the 1944 Education Act seemed to many people, a quarter-century later, to reflect and perpetuate outdated class divisions in English society. A new model was proposed: the "comprehensive school", in which children of all backgrounds and abilities were educated together, according to their needs. First steps towards a comprehensive system were taken by the Labour government of 1964–1970, and the necessary legislation was passed on Labour's return to power in 1974. The Direct Grant Grammar Schools (Cessation of Grant) Regulations, 1975 required direct grant schools to choose whether to become LEA-maintained comprehensive schools or independent schools without grant. Most direct grant schools, including WGS, chose independence. WGS had already had to readjust to some extent to the new situation, since in 1972 Manchester LEA ceased to take up places at the School. This was not too serious a blow because population drift from Manchester to Sale, Altrincham, Cheadle and beyond had made it difficult to find 35 Manchester girls among the top 65 in the School's entrance examination, and fewer were offered places. The Cheshire LEA funded a greater number of free places, compensating for the lack of Manchester funding. But the 1974 legislation forced a decision. WGS set up a Trust Fund to help less affluent families with fees, and to support building works. Some public money still came the way of the School, as, for instance, through the Assisted Places scheme introduced by the Conservative government in 1981. But, once again, WGS was independent.

While the major impact of all these changes was on the School's status and means of funding, another important effect was the need to align the Juniors' Form structure with that of the State sector. In 1973 Miss Hulme added a Transition class, introducing the Junior School structure which exists to the present day.

The developments of the 1970s inhibited WGS's building plans, but, once life had settled down, more extensions followed: new laboratories in 1977–1978, a fine new Assembly Hall cum Arts Centre in 1982 (renamed 20 years later in Miss Hulme's honour), and a further supply of classrooms from 1985. All the School's buildings stretched out north and south along the eastern edge of the site, adjoining Wellington Road, so as to leave untouched the playing fields to the west. The 1985 improvements included a dignified new entrance to what was a somewhat miscellaneous assemblage of buildings.

"Lacrosse I loved for the anarchy of having no field lines and the idea that you could run forever" (Fran Barnard (Hobson)).

Withington Juniors

WGS began as a secondary school at which pupils from Lady Barn School could continue their education. In 1919, when many important matters were under consideration, notably the purchase of the school buildings in Wellington Road, there was some talk of combining the two schools. Lady Barn House would have become WGS's preparatory department, but was too far away for this to be practicable. Until 1924 a number of girls entered the main school at age 13, but by 1924 the normal entry age had settled at 11 and WGS had three Forms accommodating girls of ages eight to ten. From then on, this remained the usual arrangement.

The younger Forms have never been physically or spiritually separated from the rest of the School. As WGS grew, classes had to be fitted to rooms as necessity required, and while the younger girls had Form mistresses, they were taught by mistresses from throughout the School, as seemed appropriate. The mistress in charge of Form 2 had always been regarded informally as the Head of Junior Department, which by 1944 had six staff. After that year's Education Act the Department was officially named the "Lower School", becoming known as the "Junior School" in the 1980s. In official *Newsletter*s, the activities of the lower Forms were usually passed over in silence until 1985, after which there was an annual report on their interesting events.

The age at which girls entered the Lower School varied. In 1973, Miss Hulme started a Transition class for girls aged seven to eight, and they joined Form I, Lower II and Upper II classes, completing what was later to become known nationally as Key Stage 2. Miss Hunter and Mrs Williams (respectively Head of Juniors and Year 5 teacher at this time) gave their names to the two junior Houses, Hunter and Williams. Mrs Hilary De Maine was appointed Head of Junior School in 1982, and Mrs Kathryn Burrows in 2005.

As activities multiplied at Withington at large, the Lower School developed its own variants – such as, from the 1970s onwards, plays written by Sybil Morton and home-grown musicals, written by Monica Hastings with music by Sasha Johnson Manning. There are Christmas concerts full of glitter and fun and Strawberry Serenades in summer. Trips to Chester Zoo; adventure activity weekends (including discos!) at Winmarleigh Hall; sports and clubs such as fencing and Pets Club; visits by eminent poets, including the inimitable David Horner, or the Young Shakespeare Company; Mad Science and Bible Encounter assemblies – all enrich, enliven and inspire, bringing the curriculum to life.

Today, the Junior School continues to be a vibrant, creative and enjoyable "thinking" environment for girls and an integral part of the whole school family. Juniors look to Seniors as role models and mentors across the breadth of WGS life and, in turn, contribute to the overall school ethos with their own special blend of inquisitiveness, irrepressible enthusiasm and, on occasion, the "Ahh" factor. It is fitting that Withington's 125th anniversary should be celebrated, amongst other things, with plans for brand new facilities for our Junior School.

Kathryn Burrows, Anthony Burton and Monica Hastings

I joined Withington aged 11 from a junior school in Stretford in 1974, courtesy of the government's direct grant system, the daughter of a single parent who couldn't afford the fees. My seven years at WGS, paired with my mum's nurture, were the roots of my self-esteem and the foundation of my love of life and continual learning. Miss Boucher watched over us all, I believed, right through school, taught me English for seven years and stood next to me in the school office when I opened my A-level results and showed her that I had repaid her faith, with the top grade, then A, in English Literature. She was truly awe-inspiring, in every sense the best representative of the selfless and dedicated teaching in every subject from which all of us girls benefited. To reflect back is also to have a sense of joy. God, it was fun; you actually thought that you might die laughing.

– DIANE HUGHES (1981)

WGS staff tended to stay for long periods. A cohort from Miss Bain's time serving under Miss Hulme included Miss M.M. Finney, Senior French mistress, admired for her elegance; Miss Nan McCardell, music mistress, noticeable for her expansive conducting of the choir; Miss Joyce Boucher (English), renowned for producing plays on an epic scale, involving most of the older girls in the School; the classics teachers Mrs P. Hill, whose mind was replete with quotations, and Miss Amy Morris, whose enthusiasm for extra-curricular activities continues in her support for Alumnae affairs; and Mrs Marjorie Rawsthorn, who brought humour and a sense of connection with everyday life into her teaching of chemistry.

Miss Hulme retired on 18th December 1985. Many commended her "remarkable ability to recognise and know every girl in the school"; while her Chairman of Governors, Dr Vincent Knowles, paid tribute to her "capacity to anticipate the future and to provide for it".

In 1990 Miss Hulme was to reveal her capacity too to reflect on the past, with her comprehensive history of the School's first 100 years. Written to mark the Centenary, the history has done much to enhance the School's knowledge and understanding of itself.

A successor to Miss Hulme was found from among WGS's existing staff. Mrs Margaret Kenyon had been on the staff since 1983 as Head of the French department. She had grown up in Liverpool, attending Merchant Taylors' School, Crosby, and proceeded to Somerville College, Oxford. Moving to the Manchester area, she did post-graduate work at the University. After her marriage she brought up two sons and taught for a long period at Cheadle Hulme School before coming to WGS. At first, Mrs Kenyon's main task was to steer the School onwards, towards its Centenary in 1990. Like Miss Hulme, she was conscious of the School's tradition. In her words:

The School remains relatively small and achieves high standards in all it does. Our excellence in science has been recognised as the Founders would have wished, but this does not detract from our strengths in the arts. Sports and outdoor pursuits flourish. No prizes are awarded; instead all our Sixth Form leavers receive a book to commemorate their time in the School and their particular contribution to it. I am confident that the Founders would be heartened by the School as it is today.

The context in which the School flourished had, however, changed considerably. The 1980s were a period of hectic educational reform by a Conservative government intent on shaking up the state sector. In 1986 O-levels were replaced by the GCSE, which, Mrs Kenyon observed, placed "greater pressure on girls and staff", owing to "the number of deadlines

Staff in 1985. Some of those mentioned in this book are: top row, L to R: 3 Mrs Barbara Ford 4 Mrs Sybil Morton 7 Mrs Sheila Bradford 10 Mrs Monica Hastings; third row, L to R: 2 Mrs Christine Manning 5 Miss Jean Fielden 7 Mrs Jillyan Farrell 8 Mrs Ruth Lindsay-Dunn 10 Miss Abby de la Portas 11 Mrs Diane Whitehead; second row L to R: 3 Mrs Hilary De Maine 4 Miss Jane Deacon 6 Miss Joyce Boucher 7 Mrs Margaret Kenyon 8 Dr Mary McDonald 9 Miss Amy Morris 10 Miss Joan Heneghan; bottom row L to R: 5 Mrs Fiona Clucas 6 Mrs Val Hempstock. Below: Mrs Kenyon, Headmistress 1986–2000.

for coursework, the feeling of being continually assessed" and "the complexity of the examinations themselves".

The 1988 Education Reform Act introduced the National Curriculum, and tougher processes of assessment. "Whilst independent schools are not bound by the National Curriculum," Mrs Kenyon observed, "it cannot be wholly ignored. Girls entering the School at any age from the state system will expect some continuity, nor should they be offered less than the National Curriculum in any of the key areas." As an independent school, WGS was somewhat sheltered from the new drive to raise standards, but, since its academic standards were so high anyway, it did not need to worry too much.

"League tables" of school results were officially published from 1992, as part of Prime Minister John Major's "Citizen's Charter", but had already appeared in newspapers. In 1991, Mrs Kenyon was pleased to announce that in the *Daily Telegraph*'s tables WGS was top girls' school in the North of England (and eighth in the country at large). She continued to express polite scepticism as to the value of such statistics, but WGS's consistently high placings were undoubtedly encouraging.

There was every reason, then, to exult in WGS's Centenary in 1990, and vigorous celebrations took place, culminating, on 4th March 1991, in a visit by the Princess Royal. Predictably, some small girls found the immediately preceding visit by police sniffer dogs even more exciting!

The 1990 Centenary Celebrations

The Centenary Year began, as all celebrations should, with a party. On a cold January afternoon, the School somehow squeezed into the Arts Centre for a rare showing of the fragile school film from the 1930s, followed by a most interesting talk by Miss Hulme about the early years of WGS. Then there was birthday cake for everyone, made by Pat Mamelok, cake-maker extraordinary.

As the Centenary approached, we discussed how best to celebrate the achievements of the first hundred years and the special character of the School. At the same time we needed to plan for the future. The first essential was to make contact with as many former Withingtonians as possible. A comprehensive database of former pupils and staff would be needed, to supplement existing lists of Senior Club members. This was long before the Internet and social networking sites, so no easy task. A records committee led by Miss Hulme and Mrs Rawsthorn, the former Senior Mistress, assisted by Mrs Mamelok, Secretary of the Senior Club, and Miss Erica Wood constituted itself early in 1988 and set to with gusto to trace as many names and addresses as possible. This was a huge undertaking and, when invitations to a Gala Weekend planned for July 1990 were sent out late in 1989, there were over two thousand recipients. The records committee's work was to prove invaluable to the School in its future relationships with Alumnae.

At much the same time, Professor Welland, our Chair of Governors, and I took to wandering around the School's exterior, debating how best to modernise the front and our cramped facilities, both sporting and academic. Stimulated by thoughts of the Centenary, we grew ever more ambitious. Gradually a two-phase building project emerged, to be funded in part by a Centenary Appeal. Phase One would be a multi-purpose Sports Hall, which in turn would free up the old School Hall for academic development in Phase Two. Our building design consultant, Professor Welland and I drove around the region to view other sports halls, and by the summer of 1990 everything was in place for construction to begin. Phase One was completed in 1991 and Phase Two in 1993.

We were also eager to commission a piece of music or work of art as a further memento of this Centenary milestone. We decided on a work of art, which led to the idea of a Centenary Tapestry to hang on the new main staircase and be seen by everyone every day. With advice from the Whitworth Art Gallery we commissioned a weaver of international reputation, Marta Rogoyska. Her large tapestry, semi-abstract, colourful and exuberant, was unveiled in May 1990. Some of us, if not all, loved it from the start. The Junior School were inspired to produce a tapestry of their own and Sasha Johnson Manning wrote the anthem "O Light Invisible" for us. It was sung on Founders' Day, so we had our piece of music too.

Then there were the celebrations within the School. Miss Boucher, who had retired the previous year, returned to produce the Centenary Revue *Northern Lights*, a celebration in words, music and dance, with the customary huge cast and much

Emblems of the Centenary. Opposite: the cake; this page the tapestry and the Northern Lights *revue.*

improvisation from the girls themselves. It was full of colour and gaiety, with touches of solemnity, a true Boucher special. The physics department organised, on behalf of the Institute of Physics, a "Physics at Work" exhibition. Withington was the first girls' school ever to host this event, welcoming exhibitors from major local and national industries, and parties of students from more than 20 schools and colleges. Playing host to the wider world proved to be a theme of the whole year.

Our celebrations culminated in the Gala Weekend, when over a thousand Alumnae visited the School, their ages spanning more than 70 years. They were regaled with music, fine food, displays of archival photographs, a Centenary Dinner in the University of Manchester, and, above all, countless opportunities to meet up with each other and their former teachers. It was wonderful.

Margaret Kenyon

Chapter Three

1990–2015: CHANGE AND CONSTANCY

Sarah Haslam

"My 2009 Founders' Day theme of Change and Constancy was wonderfully articulated by our readers, with Frost's pausing, reflecting and moving on; Tolkien's road going ever on and on, in our case with pupils pursuing it with eager feet; and, in line with Eliot's words, we shall not cease from exploration at Withington. If you want to know where you are going, you need to know where you have come from."

— MRS JANET PICKERING, WGS NEWSLETTER, *2009*

"Change and Constancy" was the theme of Mrs Pickering's final Founders' Day in 2009, and one that sums up so well the last 25 years at Withington Girls' School: "*Change, upon which progress depends, and Constancy, the quality of being enduring and unchanging, standing firm.*"

Through the challenges and opportunities offered by new technologies, economic recession, increasing media attention and an ever-competitive marketplace, Withington has remained true to the vision of its Founders, retaining and even enhancing its special qualities as a wonderfully warm and nurturing community with learning at its centre. At the Centenary Founders' Day in 1990, led by Mrs Kenyon, the chosen theme was Tolerance, and the School continues to run on the "three Rs" – Respect for Self, Respect for Others and Responsibility – whilst the principles of having no academic prizes and learning as its own reward still run strong.

Everyone who has been involved in the School knows what a unique place it is: a school where the highest standards of academic endeavour and a love of learning combine with social conscience, a wealth of activities outside the classroom and lots of fun. It sometimes seems incredible that the girls can balance such high levels of academic achievement with participation and conspicuous success in so many other activities, but at Withington happy girls thrive on all the opportunities offered. Though sometimes a double-edged sword, the media attention which has come since the early 1990s with annual analysis of examination results and league tables has given Withington a greater profile both locally and nationally too.

WGS has emerged as one of the country's leading girls' schools. A lively, stimulating centre of excellence where aspirations are always high and achievements in all areas lead the way, it remains a community grounded in normality, proud of its rich heritage and representative of our multicultural city. Our Bursary Fund, growing out of the WGS Trust founded in 1974 by Miss Hulme, now supports the education of one in six of our senior pupils. Girls leave the School to pursue their

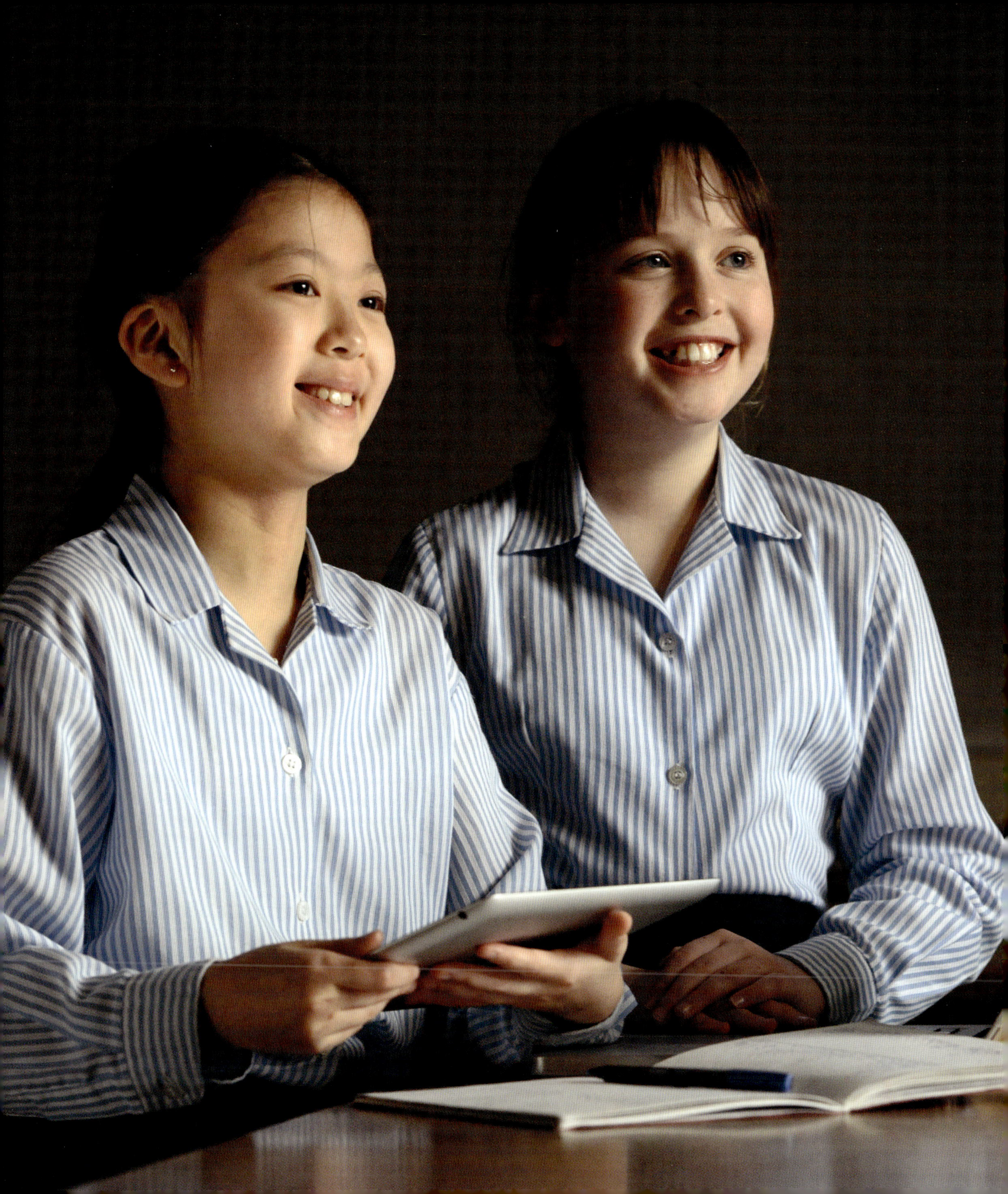

Above: Four Headmistresses celebrate Miss Hulme's 90th birthday in 2013. Clockwise from top left: Mrs Marks, Mrs Pickering, Miss Hulme, Mrs Kenyon. Below: Princess Anne's 1991 visit.

futures in a wide array of fields, equipped with that special grounding that only Withington can provide.

In 1990 the School enjoyed a wonderful year of Centenary celebrations and special musical, dramatic, sporting and artistic events. Looking back on that year, one is struck by the tremendous sense of belonging and loyalty as the community came together – girls, Alumnae, staff and former staff, parents, Governors and friends of Withington – all the result of many months of thoughtful, imaginative preparation by Mrs Kenyon, her Deputy Dr McDonald and a highly dedicated team. Intriguingly, the girls of the day were asked to imagine what a Grand Reunion of 2015 might be like, and two of their pieces are recorded in the official Centenary publication *Withington Girls' School: A celebration of the first hundred years*, written by the then Head of English, Miss Marie Green. Apart from the lack of reference to social media, which has helped more recent leavers keep in touch and could not possibly have been anticipated then, the girls' imagined accounts paint a picture many former pupils would recognise: long-lost friends thrilled to meet again, exchanging addresses and phone numbers, sharing fond memories and exploring the building, its facilities and features (including the Centenary tapestry which still hangs in pride of place above the main stairs today). The spirit of the Gala Weekend in July 1990, when over 1,000 Alumnae came back to Withington, has been rekindled many times since in events up and down the country and in school. Perhaps most special was the reunion held in March 2013 at which Miss Hulme's 90th birthday was celebrated.

The Centenary celebrations continued into 1991. In March of that year Withington welcomed HRH the Princess Royal - a fitting climax to a masterfully planned programme of events. Princess Anne's visit was designed to show her the School in action and allow everyone a glimpse of her. It took in exhibitions from the archives, the Cloud Physics Research project, the nearly completed new Sports Hall, the Junior School, the Assembly Hall where she unveiled a plaque

CHAPTER THREE • 1990–2015: CHANGE AND CONSTANCY

The Manchester Evening News *reports on the Cloud Physics Research project, 1990.*

Schoolgirls on cloud nine

OUTLOOK BRIGHT: Jane Attwell, 17, of Wilmslow, Dr Francesca Wheeler, and Lucy McLellan 17, of Marple

By Simon Spinks

GIRLS at Withington School have their heads in the clouds. And their painstaking research has turned out to have a silver lining. For the sixth form team's look at dismal weather will be seen by VIPs at a top London exhibition. They are among 18 research groups showing work at the prestigious Royal Society on June 20 and 21. The exhibition will be seen by top industrialists, education chiefs, government bigwigs, research experts and other school pupils. The Withington team have been studying the effect of pollutants on ice crystals found in thunderclouds, simulated in the lab. Another exhibit on display will show two high energy physics experiments by a group of experts from Manchester University.

commemorating her visit, and a meeting with representatives of Governors, Alumnae and parents. Three months later the completed Sports Hall was opened by Professor Welland, Chair of Governors. How fitting that Success was the theme of that year's Founders' Day.

In the early 1990s possible threats to the Government Assisted Places scheme began to emerge. The Assisted Places scheme enabled children from less affluent backgrounds

Before the Princess Royal's visit, a couple of dogs and their handlers came into school to check for bombs. Sadly they appeared at lunch time when about 500 girls were queuing or preparing to queue for lunch. Lively dogs, tails wagging wildly, were fallen upon by hundreds of doting girls all wanting to stroke and pat them. How the dogs could concentrate will never be understood and indeed perhaps they did not. They found some Cup a Soups in a desk somewhere but, of course, nothing dangerous.

– MONICA HASTINGS

to be supported financially at an independent school, transforming the lives of the Withington pupils who benefited from it. It was clear that, if the scheme were abolished, the social diversity of which Withington was so proud might be jeopardised. These were challenging times for those involved in education: the National Curriculum continued to develop, league tables became a not altogether welcome feature, debates over testing persisted and a new A* grade was introduced at GCSE. But Withington held its own throughout this period, and its reputation as a centre of excellence continued to grow: examination results were outstanding; the sporting and cultural life of the School flourished; girls travelled far and wide on school trips; three Senior School Forms replaced two; Mrs Kenyon was President of the Girls' Schools Association (1993–1994); trainee teachers learnt from the Withington staff on placement; the buildings were further expanded; and digital technology began to make its mark.

Withington has always looked to the future. When in 1997 the incoming Blair government abolished the Assisted Places Scheme, to be phased out over the following seven years, the School was prepared. Miss Hulme's foresight in establishing the WGS Trust, and its careful management by Lord Lee, meant that Withington already had funds which could partly support school places. In 2004 the Development Office was created and the first Development Director, Helen O'Donnell, a former pupil herself, was appointed. In 2005 the 100 Plus Bursary Appeal was launched, so named because its target was to raise sufficient funds (£2 million) to support at least 100 bursaries in perpetuity. From the Founders' Day of 2005, when Mrs Pickering presented the Appeal to the Withington community, the work of the Development Office gradually became an integral part of school life. Aided by Marjorie Spurgin and supported by the members of the Trust, Helen

The WGS Trust

The WGS Trust is an unincorporated charity (number 505207) governed by a Trust Deed executed in 1976. The Charity's objects are the advancement of the educational work of Withington Girls' School; charitable purposes of, or associated with, the School; and the advancement of education.

A specific aim is to maintain and enhance the level of means-tested bursary support to safeguard the diversity of the school community. In addition, the Charity provides assistance to the School in the form of grants and repayable loans to enable building projects. In the last decade, capital grants of £1.3 million have been made available to the School, helping to fund schemes such as the refurbishment and extension of the science facilities and the building of a new Sixth Form Centre.

Fundraising for the Trust is coordinated by the Development Office, and the success of its first major project – the 100 Plus Bursary Appeal – is described in this chapter. Through the Enhancing Opportunities Appeal, an annual fund established in 2012, the Charity has financed various projects to enhance girls' learning (for example purchasing a pedal harp, and a laser cutter for the design technology department). The first telephone campaign to Alumnae and parents, during the summer of 2012, raised over £110,000 for these two appeals.

Legacies are another much-valued source of funding, and in order to recognise those who would like to support the School's future in this way a legacy society (the Emily Simon Society) was formed in 2012.

The School now has a robust Bursary programme. In 2013 nearly 90 girls benefited from support, including 17 who received full bursaries, but there is clearly some way to go before the School can fulfil its long-term ambition of a needs-blind admissions process.

The Charity's Trustees have formulated their reserves policy to ensure there is adequate capital to generate sufficient income both to support Senior pupils throughout their seven-year Senior School career and to provide financial assistance for the School's building programme.

A debt of gratitude is owed to both Miss Marjorie Hulme, who was visionary in setting up the Charity, and Lord Lee of Trafford, for his unstinting work and financial acumen over almost two decades. They have done much to transform the lives of girls who have benefited from means-tested bursaries.

The Charity is deeply grateful too to all the donors who have contributed to the WGS Trust since its inception. Their gifts and legacies have been vital in helping the Bursary Fund and Annual Fund support Withington's rich learning environment.

Sharon Senn

The Margaret Connell Legacy

Margaret Connell died in October 2013, leaving a very generous legacy to the WGS Bursary Fund.

Margaret was born in Horwich in 1929 and educated at Fairfield High School and King's College, London. She taught mathematics at WGS from 1955 to 1966, encouraging many girls to study the subject at university, and went on to become Senior Lecturer at John Dalton College (later Manchester Metropolitan University). In retirement she enjoyed learning new languages, reading, music and travel. Charity was important to Margaret, and education and the opportunities it provides her passion. Her bequest will allow us to offer several full means-tested bursaries to girls for the duration of their time at the School, and will stand as lasting testament to her memory.

Sarah Haslam

O'Donnell helped raise over £1.4 million towards the Appeal, strengthened links with the Alumnae association (formerly the Senior Club, now Withington Onwards), and changed the School's fundraising culture. In 2008 the Development baton passed to another former pupil, Clare Flynn, assisted by Laura Firth, and in 2011, thanks to the immense generosity and sustained enthusiasm of the Withington community, the target of £2 million was reached.

This major milestone in the School's history was celebrated at various events, notably the Celebration Ball held at Mere Golf and Country Club, attended by hundreds from the Withington community and compèred by former pupil and the BBC's North of England Correspondent, Judith Moritz.

Today the Development Office, along with Withington Onwards, keeps some 3,000 Alumnae in touch with the School and with each other, enabling current pupils to benefit from career mentoring and networking, and playing a key role in school life as we work towards our ultimate goal of needs-blind admission.

The Ad Lucem Brick Walk (opposite) commemorates the success of the 100 Plus Bursary Appeal; a parent-teacher ensemble (above) performs at the 2011 Celebration Ball.

Judith Moritz

If light is synonymous with knowledge and understanding, then *"Ad Lucem"* is most apt to describe the career of Judith Moritz (1995 leaver). As North of England Correspondent for BBC National News, Judith has been responsible for providing the public with crucial knowledge of major events, such as the 2001 foot-and-mouth disease crisis, the Shipman Inquiry and the 2004 Morecambe Bay cockle pickers disaster, through her award-winning coverage.

Judith displayed journalistic talent early in her time at Withington; in the Lower Fourth she was amongst those who launched a student magazine, *Straight from the Horse's Mouth*. The "Grumbles Corner", covering topics such as homework and school meals, was particularly popular! In the Sixth Form, Judith developed a passion for English Literature, nurtured by Miss de la Portas, whose breadth of teaching inspired Judith to pursue the subject to degree level. Judith continued to put her love of English into practice through writing for the student newspaper while at University College London. Her entry into journalism was cemented when she was recruited as a graduate trainee for the BBC. Competition for places was fierce, but Judith credits her time at Withington for giving her "confidence, self-belief … we were taught to aim high".

In turn Judith now encourages girls at the School to aim high themselves. Speaking at the "Withington in the Media" event she gave valuable advice on how to succeed, encouraging aspiring journalists to "Go for it!"

Judith's choice of Founders' Day book was *Humanity and Inhumanity*, on the work of photojournalist George Rodger.

Vidya Ramesh

What really makes Withington tick is the unique atmosphere and the quality of the relationships amongst all parts of the community. But no school can afford to stand still where facilities are concerned, and the last 25 years have seen a number of capital projects. The Centenary appeal funded two major phases of development: first the Sports Hall and second a three-storey extension, where the Old Hall had been, with an enhanced school entrance and special facilities for science, design technology and art, geography and modern languages. These plans came to fruition in 1993 when Baroness Young opened the new extension. Interviewed by the girls for that year's *Newsletter*, the School's Caretaker Mr Garrigan talked about his "ordeal by construction" - featuring unintended triggering of the school alarm, the occasional break-in and two severings of the water mains - but his and others' pride in the finished project ("a real asset to the School") was evident. As Mrs Kenyon said in her Founders' Day speech that year, the School was "brave and bold in its planning". In 2000 ICT facilities were networked, the sports field relaid and astroturf constructed. Another major project in 2001, under Mrs Pickering's stewardship, gave us the Margaret Kenyon Wing and a host of other benefits: new Junior School facilities, including a Transition room and Resource room, which can accommodate all the Junior School for assemblies; new music rooms; a suite of English rooms; and the drama studio, named in recognition of the long-standing support given by Sir John Zochonis.

In August 2003 the School faced one of the greatest challenges of recent times when a fire destroyed the library, mathematics rooms and some of the computer facilities,

Sir John Zochonis

"Sir John Zochonis, who died in 2013 aged 84, was an industrialist whose fortune derived from African trading and Imperial Leather soap, and who quietly donated many millions to good causes in Manchester and the north-west."
(*Daily Telegraph* obituary, 15th December 2013)

Sir John was the Chair of Governors of Withington Girls' School from 1995 to 1997. A Deputy Lieutenant and former High Sheriff of Greater Manchester, he was knighted in 1997. Sir John devoted his later years to philanthropy through a charitable trust which regularly distributed more than £2 million a year. WGS was a beneficiary of Sir John's tremendous philanthropic work. Over the years he not only contributed towards new facilities for the School (including the drama studio which bears his name) but also supported the means-tested Bursary scheme, enabling bright girls to attend WGS regardless of their families' financial situation. These clever, well-educated young women are a living legacy of Sir John's generosity and commitment to education. Withington also benefited from Sir John's contribution as Governor to the shaping of the School. Margaret Kenyon, Headmistress when he was Chair, described him as "such a wise and benign presence. A great man." Amongst the many who attended Sir John's memorial service at Manchester Cathedral on 28th January 2014 were three WGS Headmistresses: Mrs Kenyon, Mrs Pickering and myself. At the invitation of his family, the lesson was read by a Withington Sixth Former.

Sir John Zochonis' philanthropic work demonstrated his true care for people. His influence is felt in many important Manchester institutions in the arts, health and education fields, and our School will be forever grateful for the support he gave us for so many years.

Sue Marks

CHAPTER THREE • 1990–2015: CHANGE AND CONSTANCY

The 2003 Fire

Mrs Pickering, Headmistress at the time, contributes an eyewitness account:

In the early hours of 23rd August 2003 I received a call from Clive Stevenson, the Premises Manager, informing me that the School was on fire. A few minutes later, as my husband and I approached Wellington Road and could see no reddening of the sky, we dared to hope that this was a minor incident. However, as we drew nearer, flames could indeed be seen coming through the roof, and seven fire tenders were already in attendance. Over the following few hours we watched the fire spread, saw at first hand courageous firefighters going well beyond the call of duty and, as a result, saving 12,000 library books from permanent damage and preventing the fire travelling the entire length of the School. We experienced the kindness of our student neighbours and appreciated the work of the Salvation Army as they supplied tea, biscuits, sympathy, hope and humour. Ever since that day the Greater Manchester Fire and Rescue Service have had free use of the School's facilities for events such as their annual Primary Schools Quiz, likewise the Salvation Army. The following few days saw the full strength of the Withington community swing into action. Governors, staff, parents and pupils, past and present, provided invaluable emotional and practical support. Girls and staff coped brilliantly with packed lunches (3,500 each week, for several weeks, made to order by the indomitable Sheena Cartledge and her team), internal water features and diversions, and Portakabins.

resulting in the flooding of the kitchen and dining rooms below. This was a moment when the Withington spirit was sorely tested but not found lacking. With all hands on deck, the efforts of staff, pupils, Governors and parents, combined with support from the architects and insurers, and, not least, the Fire Brigade, ensured that the School opened for the autumn term only two days later than planned.

The School's second experience of fire meant that Mrs Pickering's first major project, to upgrade and extend the science facilities, was delayed by one year. But as had been the case just over 40 years previously, when a fire, also caused by intruders, damaged the geography room and gym, opportunity was created from crisis and the £1 million rebuild incorporated significant improvements to the library and the mathematics classrooms. The vacated Portakabins were converted into temporary laboratories.

In 2005 the new science block opened, comprising enlarged physics and biology labs and a new Junior science lab and supporting facilities. The whole school celebrated with a designated Science Day of special activities and trips, including enthralling and informative lectures by Professor Dame Nancy Rothwell on aspects of medical research and the then Dr Brian Cox on particle physics.

Eco Warriors

The Eco Warriors come from humble beginnings: a group of Third Formers who in 2007 encouraged the School to switch off the lights. The Warriors had two forerunners, the Plant Club and World Wise, an environmentally conscious group whose guest speakers came from the Body Shop, BUAV and Greenpeace. Their demise left a gap, and the Girls' Schools Association's request that all schools achieve the Eco Schools Bronze Award provided an impetus. The newly formed Withington Eco Warriors went straight for gold, achieving the "Green Flag" Award in 2010. The scheme requires girls representing all age groups to address areas such as water, energy, waste, biodiversity and global issues. The School's curriculum and charity work were already relevant, and it went on to invest in paper recycling bins and a compactor and baler for cardboard. The Eco Warriors group raised awareness of environmental issues and planted trees, while the Juniors developed a vegetable plot and pond and took part in the RSPB Birdwatch.

Since then, the Eco Warriors have run a successful Girls Go Green Week each October, raising money for charities such as Mary's Meals; collected old clothes for the Booth Centre; and made dresses from sweet wrappers for the Fashion Show. In 2012 we were re-awarded the "Green Flag": a major achievement of which the whole school is proud.

Joanna Howling and Cristina Vilela

Three or four building projects in 20 years would be enough for most schools, but modernisation, extension and improvement did not stop there. In 2006 our multimedia Language Laboratory was opened by Professor Katharine Perera, who had retired as Chair of Governors earlier that year. The project was made possible largely by a donation of £10,000 from the School's ever-supportive Parent Teachers Association, led in recent years by Fiona Lloyd, Yvonne Dodd and, now, Joanne Kinney. The opening was the climax of a themed Foreign Languages Week featuring a lecture by Dr Penney, Fellow of Wolfson College, Oxford, and an array of cultural activities. In 2009 Mrs Pickering's final building project was completed, comprising a stunning new Sixth Form centre with state-of-the-art common room and bistro, six additional classrooms, careers room and offices and extensions to the Nurse's area and drama studio. This build incorporated many energy-saving features as part of the School's environmental commitment, which was recognised by the award of the Eco Schools Green Flag in 2010. Thanks to the vision and careful stewardship of the Governors and the building design consultants, Withington was able to make the most of its site, anticipating need and providing for all its community a bright, modern, welcoming and stimulating environment.

One of WGS's strengths must surely be that during its entire history it has had only 11 Chairs of Governors and ten Headmistresses. And successive Headmistresses have been supported by loyal, highly talented, eminently qualified and hardworking staff, all focused, whatever their area of expertise and responsibility, on the progress and wellbeing of their pupils. Dr Mary McDonald, in addition for much of the time to her responsibilities as Head of Biology, was Deputy Head for 24 of her 35 years at Withington, combining calm and compassion with supreme organisational skills and scholarship. Jillyan Farrell (now Ross) was the School's first Director of Studies for ten of her 29 years at the School, constructing numerous school timetables and overseeing curriculum development with insight and fairness, her passion for her subject always evident in her roles as Head of Chemistry and Head of Science. In her 28 years

CHAPTER THREE • 1990–2015: CHANGE AND CONSTANCY

Eco Warriors recycle sweet wrappers into dresses (above) and harvest their own veg (opposite).

as Head of the Junior School, Hilary De Maine's enthusiasm for extending young people's horizons did not diminish. She led numerous trips and activities beyond the classroom for both Juniors and Seniors, cherishing the pupils in her care and striking a balance between the new and the traditional. Monica Hastings' association with the School runs to over 40 years, as a pupil, a parent, a member of Senior Club and, of course, as a teacher, including 21 years teaching our youngest pupils, Transition. Mrs Kenyon's description of Monica as the "quintessential Withingtonian" sums up Monica's versatility, creativity and patience, all of which have benefited generations of Withington girls. Whilst it is not possible here to name all who have made significant contributions through years of service, inspiring teaching and thoughtful care, it is important to recognise that the loyalty, dedication and expertise of many staff have played a central part in the success and happiness of the School over the years. At Withington it is not only the pupils who learn; a culture of continuous professional dialogue and development, energetic commitment and reflection is part of everyday life at the School.

In the last 25 years Withington has had three Headmistresses: Mrs Margaret Kenyon (1986–2000), Mrs Janet Pickering (2000–2010) and Mrs Susan Marks (2010–); and two Heads of Junior School: Mrs Hilary De Maine (1982–2005) and Mrs Kathryn Burrows (2005–). All Heads, like all teachers, have their own style, but all Withington Heads have had in common an absolute focus on what is best for their pupils. Mrs Kenyon's retirement from Withington coincided with the millennium year, and there was a sense at the School of it being the end of an era. In 1999 Founders' Day was held for the first time at the Bridgewater Hall, and the guest speaker was Esther Rantzen, a friend of Mrs Kenyon from Oxford. On the last full day of summer term in 2000 the whole school joined together with many former pupils who returned for the occasion in a tribute Assembly full of warmth and affection. Certain key phrases summed up everyone's feelings: "She always smiles"; "she knows every girl and her parents by name"; "she makes you feel happy"; "a hard act to follow"; "outstanding". Mrs Kenyon described her Headship as "an awfully big adventure" and all were agreed that it was a challenge she had met with consummate skill, flair and style. Withington's place as one of the UK's leading academic schools was established and the stage set to meet new challenges as the 21st century beckoned.

Mrs Kenyon's successor, Mrs Janet Pickering, was brought up in the East Riding of Yorkshire and attended Bridlington High School for Girls and, in the sixth form, Malton Grammar School. She gained a first class degree in Biochemistry from Sheffield University and held research posts at the University and the Hallamshire Hospital before being appointed a Teaching Fellow at Leeds University. Following the birth of their first son, her husband Ron was appointed Head of Biology at Gordonstoun, where Mrs Pickering became a girls' house tutor and taught a sixth form general studies course, but was principally engaged with scientific publishing and editing. Following a family move south, now with two sons, as a result of her husband's appointment at The King's School, Canterbury, Mrs Pickering worked for two years updating and editing the physics and chemistry sections of *Children's Britannica* before overseeing the integration of girls into King's, running the first all-age girls' boarding house, teaching in the biology department and becoming the first female deputy Head in the School's long history. She was appointed the first female Head of St Bees, Cumbria, a co-educational day and boarding school, from where she was appointed Headmistress of Withington from September of the new millennium.

Mrs Pickering inherited an exceptional school and took it still further forward, overseeing the Bursary Appeal, extending the range of extra-curricular activities, community links and international projects, always combining a love of learning with a sense of fun. As Mrs Elisabeth Lee, Chair of Governors, put it in her *Newsletter* tribute, "Janet's enthusiasm for, and commitment to, the ethos and values of the School inspired both staff and pupils alike." The Upper Sixth girls summed it up in their choice of words for the T-shirt they presented to Mrs Pickering on their last day, declaring that she "Never … let us down". Mrs Pickering steered the School through two inspections (2001 and 2007) and introduced a number of changes to the staffing structures in line with the changing demands on schools. In 2002 the School's first Bursar, Sharon Senn, was appointed, and in 2003 Heads of Year were appointed in the Senior School. As the Independent Schools Inspectorate (ISI) commented in their 2007 report, "The pupils achieve very high levels of success and … embrace their vibrant and diverse cultural environment; their awareness of the communities in which they live and their social responsibilities are outstanding features of the school."

As Mrs Pickering's retirement approached in 2010, an atmosphere of sadness but also celebration of all that had been achieved began to pervade the School. So when in November 2009 the news came through that WGS had been named *The Sunday Times Parent Power* "Independent Secondary School of the Year 2009", it was a public recognition, if any were needed, of all that the School and its Founders valued. "Exam success is almost incidental at this school, a by-product of everything else it does – which is, of course, how it should be. The result is happy and engaged girls with a sense of purpose and a belief that they can succeed in whatever they go on to do in life" (Aliastair McCall, Editor, *The Sunday Times Parent Power*). The spontaneous cheers of delight that erupted from the girls when the announcement was made in an impromptu assembly that day said it all.

A new era began when Mrs Sue Marks succeeded Mrs Pickering in September 2010 after a rigorous selection procedure involving all Governors, many of the senior staff and some members of the Sixth Form. Mrs Marks greatly enjoyed her interview with the Sixth Form Committee – especially when she was invited to compare her leadership style to that of a certain Professor Dumbledore! Educated at Wilmslow Girls' Grammar School, she was amongst the first women undergraduates at Jesus College, Oxford, where she read Philosophy, Politics and Economics. Like her predecessor Miss Hulme, she was a rowing Blue, and she also competed for Oxford against Cambridge in

Mrs Pickering, Headmistress 2000–2010.

hockey and athletics. After Oxford, Mrs Marks first worked in the City. As a Vice President she was in charge of Bank of America's airline lending division for Europe, Middle East and Africa before changing direction in the mid-1990s after the birth of her fourth child. She took up the post of Head of Economics at St George's College, Weybridge, and after a year as Head of Sixth Form at Tormead School in Guildford was promoted to the Headship there in 2001. A strong advocate of lifelong learning, Mrs Marks gained further qualifications after taking up teaching, including an Advanced Certificate in Educational Management from Leicester University and a Certificate in Theology from the University of Exeter.

Like Mrs Pickering and Mrs Kenyon before her, Mrs Marks served on the Council of the Girls' Schools Association, first as Chair of the large South Central region and then as a member of the GSA Executive in her capacity as Honorary Treasurer. She was delighted to return, after 35 years of "exile in the south-east", to her native north-west, "which I have never stopped calling my home".

Under Mrs Marks the once experimental, now exceptional, school continues its forward momentum. The challenge of taking over responsibility for the country's Independent Secondary School of the Year might have been a daunting prospect for some, but Mrs Marks relished the opportunity to make her own contribution and began by commissioning, in the autumn term 2010, an external survey of the views of parents, pupils and staff on every aspect of school life. The feedback from this survey formed the basis for subsequent school development planning, with strong emphasis on ensuring consistency in the generally very high quality of teaching and learning, and on developing still further the excellent pastoral care provided to the girls.

The progress made by the School in these and other areas was noted by the Independent Schools Inspectorate (ISI) in their September 2013 report, which commented on further improvements made since the last inspection, in the quality of assessment, the provision of careers education and guidance, the provision of information and communication technology,

Mrs Marks, Headmistress 2010–.

the quality of governance and the quality of leadership and management. The School was rated "Excellent" in every respect, and the girls' achievements (both academic and extra-curricular) were deemed to be "Exceptional", a grade awarded to very few schools nationally.

Through all the changing years since WGS's foundation in 1890, the Founders' vision of a school which had a love of learning at its heart and sought "knowledge through difficulty rather than success through ease" (Recital of the Founders) has prevailed. Withington today is both vibrant and reflective, inclusive and diverse, principled and liberal. As Mrs Burrows so aptly puts it, Withington is a "people place". A place where the Golden Rule of Respect for Self and Respect for Others underpins all school rules, where the girls are "receptive, alert, articulate and highly motivated … confident, happy and self-reflective, with genuine concern and respect for both their peers and staff", achieving "at an exceptionally high level" and "are often bold, independent thinkers who relish discussing their ideas" (ISI Report 2013). The girls' enthusiasm for their Houses, named in the Senior School after four of the Founders, is undimmed. We hope that the Founders would be as proud of the girls as they are of them and of their School.

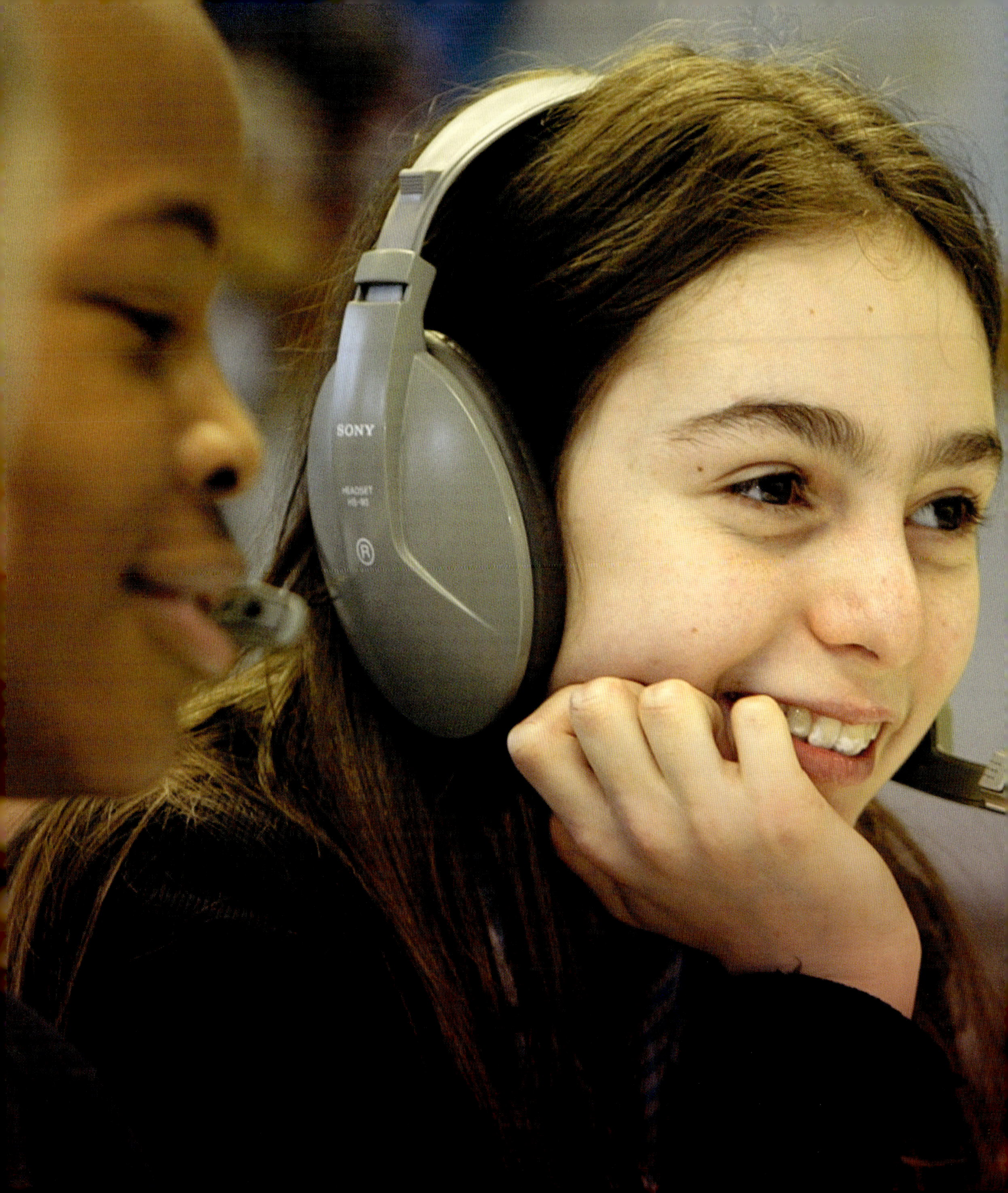
SONY

2 School Life

"We are increasingly focusing on teaching our girls to think for themselves, to challenge 'received wisdom', to work things out for themselves and not simply to become compliant followers of instructions. This model of learning pre-supposes mutual courtesy and respectfulness, of course."

– MRS SUE MARKS, HEADMISTRESS, HEAD'S LINES, WGS BULLETIN, OCTOBER 2012

Chapter Four

THE SCHOOL COMMUNITY

Christine Davies

"A school that operates as a harmonious and happy community with a minimum of rules."

– 2013 INSPECTORS

One of Withington's defining features is its sense of community and family. Since its inception the School has remained relatively small (since the 1990s stabilising at around 650 girls), making for an environment where staff know all the girls well and each pupil is encouraged to grow as a person as well as intellectually. Withington does not have an elaborate system of rules and regulations; instead the pupils are reminded in an assembly near the start of every academic year of the "Golden Rule", which governs the behaviour of all those who learn and work in the School. Based on one of the guiding principles of all major religions and belief systems, this can be summed up as "Treat others as you would like them to treat you", and it is this sense of caring for others that makes the atmosphere so positive and supportive.

The sense of "family" which permeates WGS can be seen in its most literal sense in the number of Alumnae who choose to send their daughters or granddaughters to the School. Together with the daughters, granddaughters and nieces of other Founders, the daughters of Louisa Lejeune, one of the Foundation Governors, were all educated at the school she helped establish: Franziska and Helen went on to study English at Oxford University; Marian read modern languages at Cambridge and Caroline studied English at Manchester. And so a tradition was established. Today many of the girls in the Senior School are "second generation" Withingtonians, and one girl can trace the connection back in a direct line to her great-great-grandmother!

The School has four Houses: Herford, Lejeune, Scott and Simon, named after four of the Founders. The House system began in 1925 under the headship of Miss Grant at the suggestion of Miss Corfe - who taught physical education and

Left: Form IVB, summer 1914.

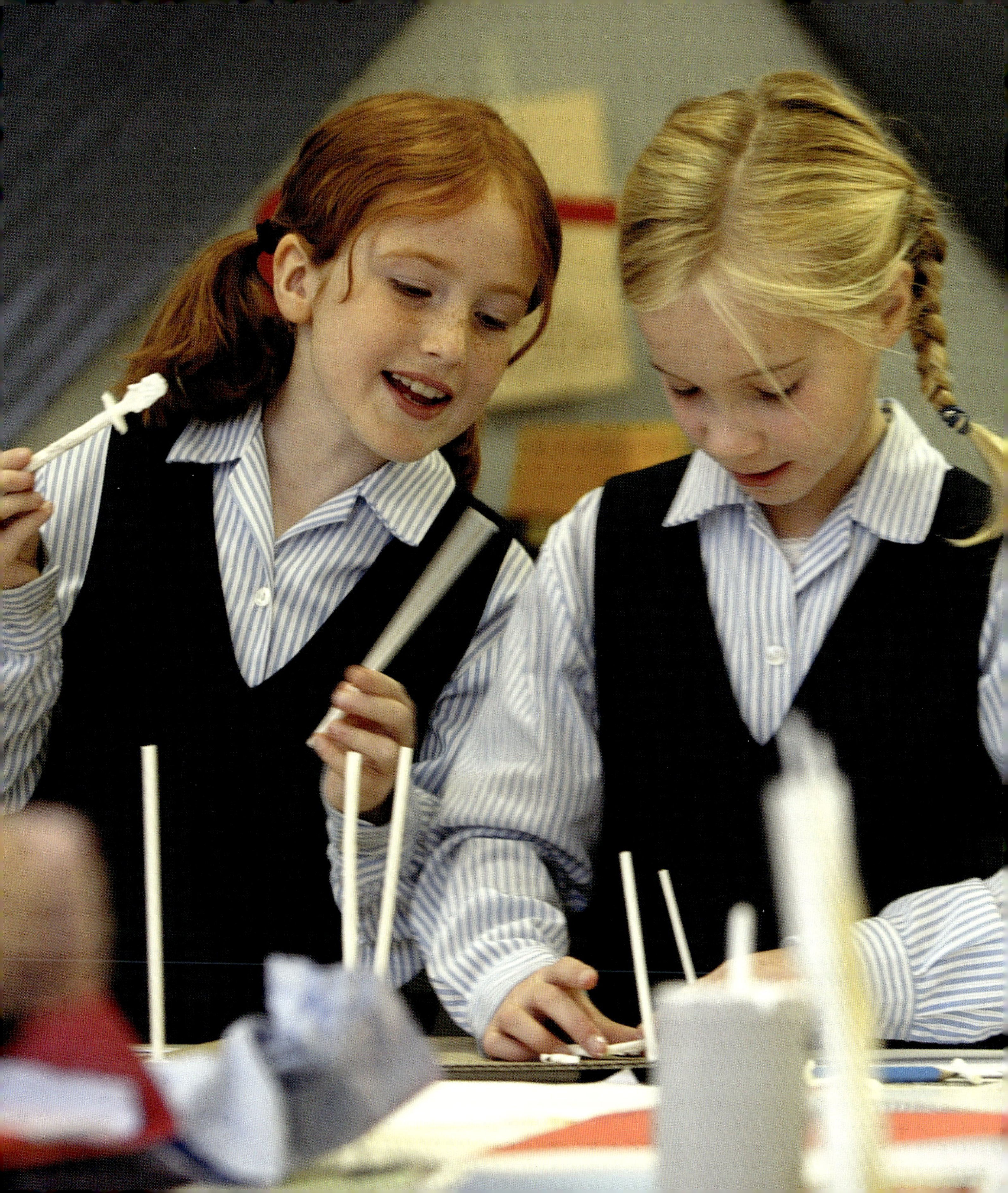

Peer Support

One of Withington's greatest achievements is the sense of community that abounds throughout the School, epitomised in the Peer Support system which operates successfully across all years.

Peer Support started in 1999 as a kind of "drop-in" clinic, where younger girls could come to Sixth Formers with any problems, and talk about a range of issues. As the system developed each Form was allocated a Sixth Former, and now has three or four Upper Sixth students who attend weekly sessions on Wednesday mornings. Each year group has offered its own challenges and rewards. The morning sessions cover a range of activities, from circle time and games in the Junior School, to quizzes and planned activities, discussions and individual conversations in Years 7–9. Peer Supporters take part in all-year group events, including Induction Day and Ghyll Head weekends, and attend Parents' Evenings, forming excellent relationships with the girls they support and acting as positive role models. In Years 10 and 11 students discuss coping with coursework and exams, what to expect in the Sixth Form, A-level subjects, and choosing and applying for university.

Students take the responsibilities attached to the role seriously and the system plays a large part in creating the "harmonious and happy community" that the 2013 Inspection Team observed. They commented on the positive relationships amongst the pupils, with older girls doing "much to help the younger ones", especially as Peer Supporters. Recent innovations include the creation of Heads of Junior and Senior Peer Support, who sit on the Sixth Form Committee. Each year group has produced a booklet offering guidance for the following year, and we look forward to the continuing development of this important part of Withington's pastoral systems.

Jude Wallis

Above and opposite: peer support in action.

games – in order to make competition fairer. Until then, Forms had played against each other at all games with pupils of all ages competing, with predictable results: the older girls always won. House events now include Sports Day, the Swimming Gala, House Plays and House Carols, with points contributing to the Summer and Winter Shields. These are always fiercely contested, with a sense of friendly rivalry spurring all girls on to do the best they can for their House.

Upon entering WGS pupils are put into a House, the same one as their older sisters, mothers, aunts or grandmothers if they are following them into the School, giving a real sense of loyalty and identity. Members of staff are also associated with a House, the same one they were in as a pupil, if they are an Alumna, and the same as their daughter if she is a pupil. For many teachers therefore there is a huge emotional investment in their House, and they can be seen waving their scarves in the House colours of green, red, blue or yellow with as much enthusiasm as the girls on Sports Day or during the House Plays. The Heads of House are responsible for organising

CHAPTER FOUR • THE SCHOOL COMMUNITY

activities throughout the year and it is in these events that the true community spirit of WGS can be seen. Every Christmas the Arts Centre resounds to the sound of singing as the House Carol competition brings the whole school together to support their House. Sixth Form House Committee members write the music and the words of a carol and, after some judicious editing by staff, teach these to the younger girls. The atmosphere is truly exhilarating, with the performers being cheered on by the whole school. In the summer this is repeated with the House Play competition, which again ends the term on a note of supportive rivalry. The summer term also brings Sports Day, when the whole school as well as many parents and other supporters set off in buses for Longford Park to marvel at the levels of skill and strength in girls of all ages. The Swimming Gala is another opportunity for pupils to display their sporting prowess, although it is also often remembered because members of the committee of the winning House (and sometimes the teacher who is Head of House) usually end up being thrown in the pool.

The House system is not the only way a sense of community is engendered at WGS; older pupils have a great deal of responsibility for the younger girls in both formal and informal contexts. Upper Sixth Formers are elected to responsible positions: in addition to the Head Girl and her Deputies, there are the Sixth Form Committee, Heads of Religious Societies and House Captains, all of whom have a special part to play in the running of the School. The Sixth Form Committee meets regularly, alongside Form representatives, with senior members of staff in School Council and Feedback (Catering Committee) to discuss a range of issues, most of which have been tabled by the pupils themselves. In this way the student body's voice is heard, and many of the pupils' suggestions have been implemented as school policy. Popular topics for discussion include homework, school lunches and the buses! The Head Girl and Deputies of course play a key role in this, but also represent WGS on other occasions, such as on Founders' Day, or when visitors require a tour of the School. They also lead assemblies at various times throughout the school year.

Every member of the Upper Sixth has the opportunity to become a Peer Supporter. Peer Supporters are attached to younger Forms and not only help keep them entertained by organising games and quizzes but also offer valuable advice and guidance from the perspective of someone who knows the challenges of school life and has been through each stage themselves. The Sixth Formers are given training to help them carry out this vital role and frequently provide a "listening ear" for younger girls with particular anxieties.

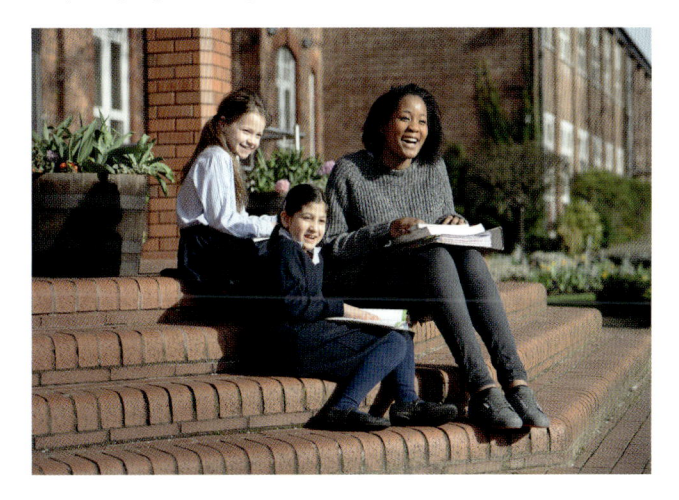

> *In the 1960s we did everything we could to make the uniforms as unrecognisable as possible. We hated the hat, a compulsory soft velour, and rolled and squashed it to minimise it, then pinned it on the back of our heads as far out of sight as possible. The mini skirt was all the rage and I recall having to kneel down for a "hem inspection" by a member of staff. Hems were to be no more than 4 inches off the ground – but they were fighting a losing battle until the maxi came into fashion!*
>
> – RUTH MORGAN (PIMLOTT) (1968)

WGS has a network of supporters who expand the school community into the wider local environment. The Governing Body, comprising parents, Alumnae and friends of the School, has always supported the endeavours of staff and pupils in terms of approving policy and offering guidance. In recent years the role of the Governing Body has evolved and developed: in 2009 members became more involved in the School's day-to-day life by being attached to an academic department or departments; each Governor visits lessons in their chosen subject areas, speaks to Heads of Department, teachers and girls and therefore gets a real sense of what life is like for staff and pupils and what particular challenges each

> *Staff too in the 1950s were given a taste of uniform, since they were expected to wear gloves on their way to school.*
>
> – MISS MORRIS

Above: the 2014 Spring Fair in full swing. Right: uniforms in the 1970s.

The electric bell was introduced about 1942. Before that the Lower Fifth girls regulated the school day by dashing round the School ringing a hand bell - the kind used by Town Criers - to indicate the end of one lesson and the start of the next.

– MORAG MERICA (McCAIG) (1945)

department faces. The ongoing partnership provides support and advice for staff while allowing Governors to extend their active role in the school community. To further the connection, members of staff with responsibility for a particular subject area or initiative often present their ideas to the Governors, allowing for greater knowledge and understanding on both sides, and, since Mrs Pickering's tenure as Headmistress, members of the Senior Management Team have attended Governors' meetings and made significant contributions to their areas of responsibility.

The PTA has long provided an opportunity for parents to play a larger role in the life of the School and continues to go from strength to strength, each year exceeding its own impressive records. Amongst other fabulous achievements, the PTA has recently raised sufficient funds to purchase a new school minibus. The annual PTA Ball is a truly spectacular event, raising thousands of pounds for WGS and its associated charities, and PTA members also organise the Spring Fair, where the whole school comes together with each Form manning stalls offering games, cakes and raffles. The day before the Spring Fair is traditionally a non-uniform day where pupils can wear their own clothes for school – as long as they bring a donation of a prize for the Fair's tombola stall. The PTA also benefits from the sale of second-hand school uniforms. In 2008 the uniform changed to include a jacket and a pleated skirt, creating a more professional image and adding to the School's sense of community.

As in all schools, life at Withington has a daily, and a yearly, rhythm, and it is partly the growing familiarity with these rhythms that helps girls feel a sense of belonging and a sense of

Clockwise from top left: a religious studies class; Harvest Festival (with the Junior School's Centenary tapestry in the background); baking bread for Mitzvah Day.

identity. Upon arriving at WGS girls quickly come to identify strongly with their Form. Under the guidance of their Form teacher they organise charity events, discuss pastoral issues and participate in activities such as "Secret Santa". The Form room gives girls a base where they can chat, do homework and relax at breaks and lunchtimes.

Assemblies take place three times a week; two of these are opportunities for the whole school to meet and consider topical issues which can vary from the achievements of Alan Turing to the importance of being resilient, and from philosophy to physics. WGS prides itself on being a place which welcomes girls of all faiths or of none, and once every week girls meet in their faith groups – Christian, Jewish, Muslim, Hindu or secular – to worship and discuss issues of importance to them. Important religious festivals of all faiths are marked in whole-school assemblies where girls of a particular religion share with the rest of the students their beliefs and the ways they celebrate them. Holocaust Memorial Day has been marked in recent years by the visit of a Holocaust survivor – a humbling and moving experience for the whole school.

When she became Headmistress, Mrs Marks quickly established the tradition that every Form should organise and present an assembly once a year. The girls choose the topic themselves, often supporting their presentations with music, video clips and PowerPoints. Recent topics include "Sleep", "Disney" and "Halloween".

The Harvest Festival has long been a feature of the WGS calendar. In recent years girls have been asked to provide tinned food and dry goods which are donated to the Booth Centre, a walk-in centre for the homeless based in Manchester

CHAPTER FOUR • THE SCHOOL COMMUNITY

The school day starts with registration in your Form room with your Form teacher then you have a thought-provoking assembly or Peer Support session. All this is before the two first lessons of the day. Then you have break. You can choose from a wide range of food such as crisps, bagels and home-made cakes. Two more lessons follow and then it's lunchtime, when there is a variety of sports to do such as lacrosse and netball as well as many non-sporting activities. The last four lessons are after lunch, and at 3.45 it is time to go home, or you could always attend an after-school rehearsal or play in a match.

– TARA POWER, IIIY

"I loved school especially for the games, my friends and the school puddings" (Fran Barnard (Hobson)). Top: lunchtime; bottom: the Sixth Form common room.

Cathedral. On these occasions representatives of the Centre have spoken at the service about their work and shared some of their visitors' case studies. This is always a humbling experience, reminding us all of the harsh economic situations faced by so many people in our city.

The main event in the school year is Founders' Day in October, when staff, present and past pupils, parents and friends of WGS gather to remember the School's foundation and the principles of the Founders – as important now as they were then. Founders' Day follows a familiar pattern, with music and readings, speeches and hymns, and of course the presentation to girls in the Upper Sixth of a book of their choice. Always there is the singing of the school song, "Gaudeamus", and the recitation of the Founders and their principles. As pupils progress through the School, this becomes an event which characterises the school year and which is looked back on with a sense of nostalgia in years to come (see also Chapter 1).

Christmas is a time when the whole school comes together to celebrate and rejoice. In early December the tree in the Arts Centre is decorated and a number of musical activities follow in quick succession. Every year the School organises a party for elderly members of our local community, which involves singing along with familiar carols and songs, party food and, of course, games. For many, this is the highlight of the school year, with a true Christmas spirit and a genuine sense of fun (see also Chapter 9).

"Gaudeamus"

Gaudeamus igitur, Juvenes dum sumus;
Post jucundam, juventutem, Post molestam senectutem
Nos habebit humus!

"Gaudeamus Igitur" (also known as "De Brevitas Vitae" – on the shortness of life) is a popular academic "commercium" song in many European countries, meaning it is sung at formal ceremonies such as university graduations and special academic feasts. Despite this formal usage, it is a jocular, light-hearted composition that pokes fun at university life. Based on a Latin manuscript from 1287, the song dates from the early 18th century. With its exhortations to enjoy life, it evokes the importance of *carpe diem* (seizing the day).

"Gaudeamus" was always known as a rousing song in its own right, and its joyous and positive sentiments made it a popular choice for many academic institutions. Miss Bain, who became Withington's Headmistress in 1938, decided it would be an excellent choice, too; and it has been our school song ever since. Withingtonians have sung, and continue to sing, their beloved song all over the place. From Ghyll Head to Kilimanjaro, the strains of "Gaudeamus" will unite everyone fortunate enough to have had the Withington experience.

Sasha Johnson Manning

Autumn Term : Founders' Day

1 Gaudeamus igitur

Old German Students' Song

Gau-de-a-mus i-gi-tur, Ju-ve-nes dum su-mus;
Post ju-cun-dam, ju-ven-tu-tem, Post mo-les-tam se-nec-tu-tem
Nos ha-be-bit hu-mus, Nos ha-be-bit hu-mus!

2 Vivat academia,
Vivant professores,
Vivat membrum quodlibet,
Vivant membra quaelibet,
Semper sint in flore.

3 Vivat et respublica,
Et quae illam regit,
Vivat nostra civitas,
Maecenatum caritas,
Quae nos hic protegit.

Translation of Gaudeamus

So let's be happy, then
While we are young.
After the pleasures of youth,
After the problems of old age,
The earth claims us.

2 Long live school!
Long live the teachers!
Long life to each one of us
Long life to all of us,
May we always give our best.

3 Long live our Country, too,
And she who reigns over it,
Long live our Community,
And the generosity of our benefactors
That protects us here.

CHAPTER FOUR • THE SCHOOL COMMUNITY

Awe-inspiring, academic and simply magnificent, were my first thoughts and feelings as a privileged newcomer. Navigating through this hub of learning became easier after the second day. There were many new things to explore but I liked the science laboratories. The first thing I enjoyed was deciding which extra-curricular activities I wanted to attend from the abundance on offer.

– HUMNA AMAR, IIIX

The Christmas Concert is an opportunity for WGS musicians to display their talents. A recent tradition is the inclusion of *The Twelve Days of Christmas* with full audience participation. It is difficult to remain aloof while miming "Eight geese a-laying", and the whole audience is soon up on its feet amongst laughter and song. A more sombre mood is evident in the traditional Carol Service at St Ann's Church in Manchester; here, members of the school community come together to sing carols and listen to the nine traditional lessons, the sign for many that Christmas has truly begun.

For many years now Withington has held an Entrance Examination in January where ten- and 11-year-old girls from the Junior School and other primary schools come into School to sit examinations in English and mathematics. The staff try to make this as pleasant an experience for the young applicants as an examination can possibly be, helped by Third Form girls who act as guides and runners for the day. This is a defining moment in the life of a Third Former – a time when she is deemed to know the School well enough to take on the role of an expert and offer advice and help to others. Upon entering WGS, many pupils remember the girls from the year above who helped them on the day of their Entrance Examination, and connections across year groups are established and strengthened.

Christmas rituals. Top: the Junior School play; bottom: the St Ann's Carol Service.

Sixth Form leavers' Cirque du Withé in 2013.

As the school year moves to its end girls are involved in examinations – external examinations for the older pupils and school examinations for the others – followed by the House Plays and either the Festival of Spoken English and Drama or the Music Festival, biennial events which alternate. All too soon it is time for the last day of the year and Final Assembly. This celebrates the achievements of that year: sporting, musical, dramatic and academic, individual as well as collective. It is also when the names of the girls who will hold positions of responsibility the following year, including Head Girl and Deputy Head Girls, are announced. These names are kept strictly secret until the final day of term and the tension in the room when they are read out is palpable. At the end of Final Assembly "Go Forth with God" is sung with much emotion, especially from the Upper Sixth for whom it marks their last day at school. Alumnae often comment that they cannot hear that hymn without it bringing a tear to their eyes! Fortunately, soon after leaving, pupils are invited back for a tea party where they can say a more measured farewell to their teachers and discuss their preparations for university.

Alumnae of the School join Withington Onwards, formerly the Senior Club. This association was founded very soon after the School, and was certainly well-established by 1902, when its members put on a play to entertain pupils. Since then it has gone from strength to strength, maintaining links with ex-pupils and forming an important part of the school community. There is a full programme of reunions and events targeting year groups or larger groups of Alumnae, a dedicated section of the WGS website and an annual publication keeping members informed of School events. The loyalty felt by Withington's Alumnae was demonstrated in 1990, when at the time of the Centenary over 1,000 ex-pupils visited the School for a Gala Weekend. Worldwide there are over 3,000 members of Withington Onwards who continue to support WGS by their contributions to the Bursary Fund and the more recent Enhancing Opportunities Annual Fund which has raised money for specific projects within the School.

Life in Withington was nothing I expected it to be. Every moment is different, every experience is memorable. The first day was scary. I didn't know anybody and I couldn't find my way around the School. Already after the third day, I felt I had been there for a long time. It has been a great term and highlights have been Ghyll Head and Founders' Day. However, the best things of all are my new friends. Now I am already feeling I am going towards the light … Ad Lucem.

– KATRIN JIVKOVA, IIIW

CHAPTER FOUR • THE SCHOOL COMMUNITY

Alumnae meet up again at Withington Onwards gatherings.

In 1924 C.P. Scott spoke of the School's aims at Founders' Day. His comments were recorded in the *Manchester Guardian*:

It was felt ... that education, to be of value, should be valued by the child, and that the child should be interested in its work. So far as the good schools were concerned the old idea that the child went unwillingly to school was exploded. It was now realised that if the teaching was good the child would love it, and that it could only appeal to the child if the child was made to understand what it was doing from the very beginning.

Along with the other guiding precepts of the Founders, this is as true of Withington Girls' School today as it was then. Pupils are made to feel part of the process, part of the community, and it is this which accounts for the enduring success of the School and the positive and friendly atmosphere commented on by all who study or work at WGS or who have reason to visit.

69

Chapter Five

ACADEMIC LIFE

Ian Mckenna

"If it is to work well, the mind must be stretched by the stimulation of interest and this is inherent in good teaching."

– MISS MARJORIE HULME, WGS *NEWSLETTER*, 1977

While much of what makes Withington special happens outside the classroom, like any school its academic life is integral to its character. The Founders' vision largely defined the type of school WGS is, but its social, political and educational context has inevitably shaped the ways the founding aims could be fulfilled.

This brief view of academic life at Withington focuses on the recent past. Part 1 of this book outlines the early development of the curriculum, and Miss Hulme's history of the School and the *Celebration of the first hundred years* provide further detail. Since they were written, secondary education has changed significantly in the UK. GCSEs, designed to combine O-levels and the lower-level CSEs into a single qualification to be sat by all pupils at the age of 16, were introduced shortly before WGS's Centenary. It is a truth universally acknowledged among more experienced teachers that educational fashion is cyclical, and indeed at the time of writing GCSEs are due in their turn to be replaced by something more akin to O-levels.

So this chapter covers the lifespan of GCSEs: lauded by some as providing a standardised way of assessing the achievements of all secondary school pupils, but increasingly criticised in the popular press for "dumbing down" academic standards and giving pupils multiple attempts to pass examinations by re-sitting papers as many times as necessary. Some of the same criticisms have been levelled at the modular system of AS and A2 levels that replaced the traditional linear A-level qualifications in the government's Curriculum 2000 initiative.

Whether this is true or not has mattered little at Withington, as both teachers and pupils aim not only to be thorough in their study of any subject (academic thoroughness being identified by the Founders as "the first condition of real progress") but also to go beyond the requirements of examination specifications. Another of the Founders' key stipulations was that "The endeavour will be to make the work of the School interesting and stimulating in itself, rather than to depend on examinations and prizes as motives to exertion." While it is undeniable that pupils' examination achievements are a notable feature of Withington's success, its ethos has remained true to the original aspiration and it has sought much more than examination success.

"The world is full of magic things, patiently waiting for our senses to grow sharper" (attributed to W.B. Yeats).

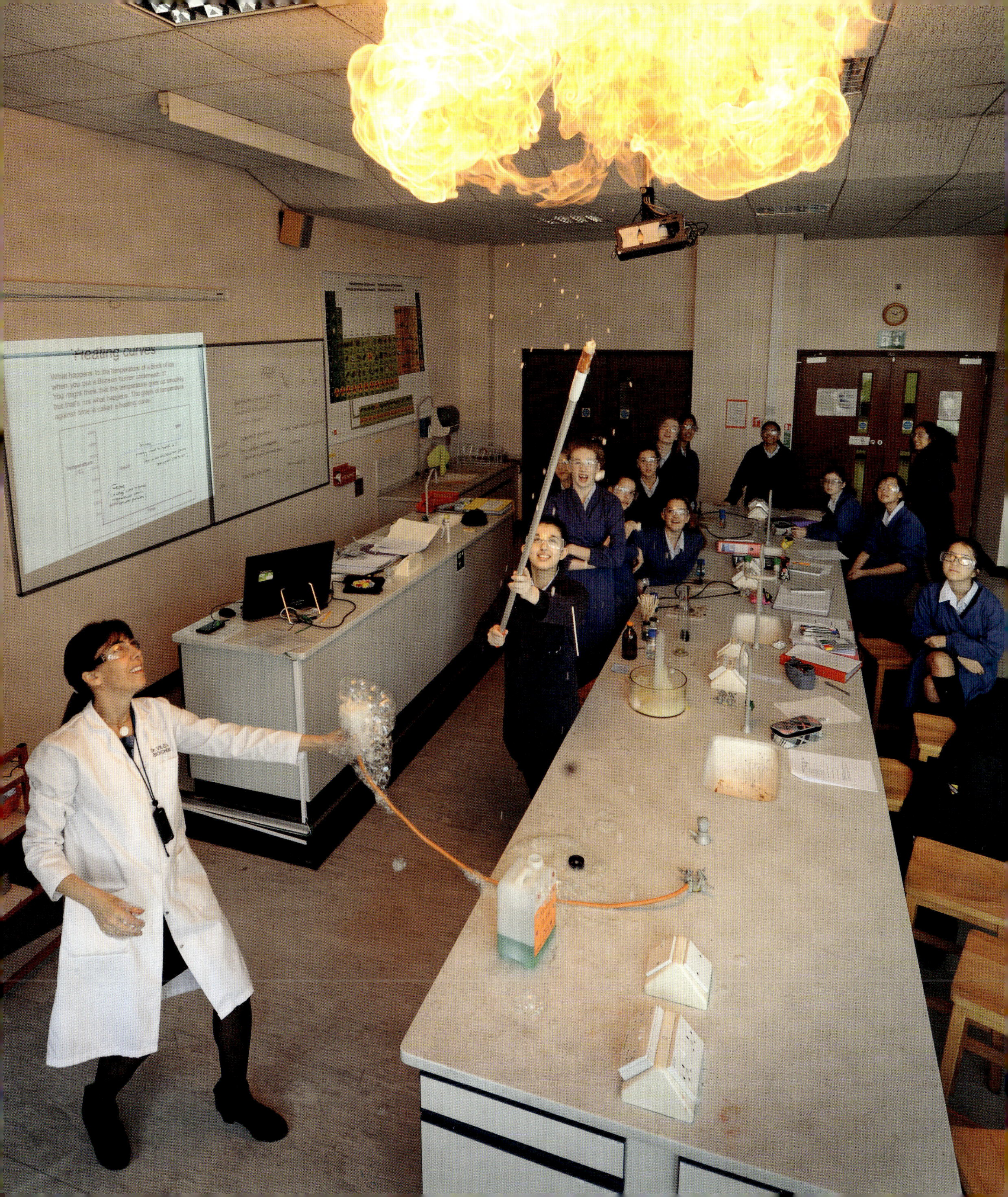
Heating curves

Learning about the world in the early 1950s and the 2000s.

Former Head Girl and current Head of Geography Julie Buckley remembers as a pupil learning in a serious, focused and disciplined atmosphere, but also being allowed to explore, thanks to teachers' warmth and enthusiasm, academic issues far beyond the requirements of curriculum or examinations. The ability and willingness of both pupils and teachers to engage with subjects for their own sake is one of the most enjoyable aspects of the classroom experience at WGS. Questions arising are discussed simply because they are fascinating, while focus can quickly be brought back to the original aims and objectives of the lesson. Mutual confidence – of pupils in their teachers' expertise and of teachers in their pupils' maturity – is one of the factors that make academic life at the School so successful.

Withington girls all currently spend part of their week in lessons that either develop awareness and skills or explore ideas simply because these are valuable things to do, and not because there is an examination to be sat at the end of the course. Lower and Upper Fifth Formers explore the development of key ideas in human history in religion and philosophy lessons and Upper Fifth Formers take brief courses in art appreciation, sports leadership, critical thinking and study skills. Sixth form students attend general studies lessons in addition to their other A-level classes, and then have the option of whether or not to take the general studies examinations at the end of Upper Sixth. Personal, social, health and citizenship education is a well-established part of the curriculum and helps to prepare girls for life outside school.

A look at the grades achieved by Withington girls in any year demonstrates that this freedom to explore issues beyond the syllabus does not compromise their success in external examinations. It is recognised that high grades are important as they allow the girls to go on to study at top universities, which they almost all do. The girls' examination results have always been excellent, and in spite of the shortcomings of league tables as a measure of how good a school is, it is gratifying that they invariably show that WGS earns the highest academic results north of Oxford. Although none of Withington's Headmistresses since the inception of league tables in 1992 especially values them, Mrs Pickering does believe that their initial publication led to increased national recognition of the School's excellence.

In addition to changes in the format of public examinations and the publication of school league tables, a major development in education over the last 25 years is the

CHAPTER FIVE • ACADEMIC LIFE

more demanding school inspection system. Like many other independent schools, WGS has since 2001 been inspected by the Independent Schools Inspectorate, whose most recent visit to the School in September 2013 resulted in a superb report, with Withington being awarded the highest grade in every section. It was particularly rewarding to hear that the pupils' academic achievements were judged to be "Exceptional", an accolade conferred upon very few schools nationally: "The quality of the pupils' achievements and learning is exceptional. Pupils receive an outstanding education in accordance with the school's aims to help girls achieve an excellent standard of academic achievement, and to foster an intellectual curiosity, a love of learning, independence of mind and individual responsibility."

Part of the inspection process involves an intensive schedule of lesson observations, which has become a much more integral part of teaching over the last couple of decades. In many schools, a teacher's classroom had historically been regarded as sacrosanct; it was their private domain in which they alone judged how best to impart knowledge to their charges. This is not to say that teachers did not collaborate with each other, nor that nobody aside from the individual teacher

Laura Carstensen

Laura Carstensen, Commissioner at the Human Rights and Equality Commission, left WGS in 1979. English literature was and is Laura's subject and her passion. At Withington her English teacher, Joyce Boucher, "spotted and nurtured my talent for the subject even though she undoubtedly found me infuriating and we could not have been more unlike as people". Shakespeare was a golden thread for Laura, running through every year from the Third Form to the Upper Sixth; she could still tell you which plays she studied, probably in the right order! The belief that achievement is its own reward, and the assumption that girls and women can succeed and should be seen to succeed in all areas, have really inspired Laura, particularly when she began studying English at Oxford. When she started work in City law in 1985, the lack of women in that area intensified her motivation and she went on to become an equity partner in 1994, leaving the City ten years later to pursue a portfolio career. Laura loved the intellectual challenge that competition law gave her with its fusion of economics, law and public policy; the oral advocacy that indulged her love of words; and the adrenalin rush of deals that made the financial news. Those 20 years were the basis for everything else since. Laura now lives on a mountain in the north Welsh borders, travelling as needed. She reckons she has the near-ideal balance, working in London and from home, with time to indulge her love of reading. Laura's choice of Founders' Day book? *Fifty Years of Vogue Fashion Photography*.

Julia McCarthy

Bridget Eickhoff

Bridget Eickhoff left Withington in 1974. She is currently working for the RSSB (Rail Safety and Standards Board) as Principal Infrastructure Engineer, having served a term in 2012 as Chairman of the Railway Division of the IMechE (Institution of Mechanical Engineers). Bridget's interest in engineering stemmed from the practical toys she and her brother played with as children, such as Lego and Meccano. But she never put a name to the discipline until she went on to study maths at university after her A-levels – choosing *Mathematical Models* by H.M. Cundy and R.P. Rollett as her Founders' Day book. Bridget says that university maths was very different from school maths, and much harder, but once she realised her passion lay in engineering and she was offered a job in that field, she never looked back. Bridget has had a wide range of responsibilities in the engineering profession, such as development, communication and team management. Her work has benefited rail networks in Great Britain and Europe, as she has contributed to many of the safe, cost-effective railway systems we all use today. She looks forward to continuing her work and facing the many technical challenges that come with railway engineering.

Natalie Wynn

The staff room in 1953.

and their pupils knew what went on in lessons, but there was much less scrutiny and consequently fewer opportunities for teachers to learn from each other and share good practice.

Happily, this attitude is increasingly rare and certainly goes against the grain at WGS. Over time, teachers have become much more aware of the value both of observing colleagues teaching and of being observed in turn by colleagues, who are then in a position to offer constructive advice on how to improve. This most valuable of professional practice is becoming more and more embedded in the culture at Withington, not just when inspections take place, but as a matter of course.

While for teachers and students the inspection process is a stressful one, it has contributed to at least three positive trends: first, schools have been encouraged to become more collaborative places; second, they are now more proactive about teachers' professional development; and third, they have become more rigorous in ensuring that each pupil's individual educational needs are met.

With regard to the first of these points, several long-serving teachers at Withington have noted that academic departments are now much more cohesive than they were in the past, with ideas, resources and tasks more readily shared between departmental staff, and the pupils' experience consequently more consistent regardless of which class they are in. Some may mourn the passing of an age when more teachers were what might be described as eccentric, and certainly homogeneity in itself is no virtue, but there is surely a value in teachers learning from each other (and indeed from their pupils) about what helps young people learn most effectively.

A second positive trend concerns in-service training days (more recently referred to as continuing professional development, or "CPD", days), which have become a key feature of teaching since they were introduced in 1988 by the then Education Secretary, Kenneth Baker. WGS staff have four CPD days each year, with roughly half the time spent on training in pastoral issues and half devoted to academic matters. This is redolent of another of the Founders' aims, namely that the School's teachers should have strong academic and professional qualifications. This has always been the case at Withington, but the staff have become increasingly aware in the latter part of the School's history that qualifications must be supplemented by ongoing professional training. We have for many years supported trainee teachers through our partnership with the University of Manchester, and in addition run termly training days on behalf of the Independent Schools Teacher Induction Panel for those in their first year of employment. This involves welcoming up to 40 visiting teachers from across the north-west and sometimes beyond to a stimulating day of activities and reflection run by a team of committed WGS staff, led by Deputy Head Sarah Haslam and Head of the Junior School Kathryn Burrows.

The third and most important trend in teaching in the last 25 years is the greater awareness of the fact that each child is an individual who learns in their own way, and who may have certain learning difficulties that require different strategies on behalf of the teacher. This requires two things: ways for teachers to assess the needs of each child, and the means to offer support for those who need it.

The first kind of individual support for girls with educational needs at Withington was offered by Elinor Chicken and Anna Godwin, who still does excellent work with girls today. Elinor and Anna began to identify girls for

Lesley Cohen

Lesley Cohen is Professor of Solid State Physics at Imperial College, London. She left Withington in 1980, having followed her older sister, Michelle, into the School. She remembers being proud, as a Junior, of having a big sister in the Senior School! Lesley enjoyed all her subjects for the first five years and remembers Miss Boucher's English lessons with great affection. However, it was in the sciences that her passion lay, and she describes Miss Mercer's experiments as "a marvel". At A-level, physics and mathematics were equally absorbing, but the connection physics made with the real world was a deciding factor, and thus Lesley went on to study the subject at Bedford College, London. Lesley is constantly inspired by her work as a physicist; she is fascinated by the interactions that take place within exotic materials such as ferromagnets and superconductors, and constantly excited by the way her research can lead to technological breakthroughs in areas as diverse as ultra-sensitive chemical detection and materials for energy-efficient use. Having been inspired by the teachers at Withington, Lesley now enjoys working with gifted young people and guiding them through their own love of physics.

Christine Davies

whom spelling was an issue, and ran sessions to help them outside lessons; this was later expanded to include support with language learning. Elizabeth Robinson took over this responsibility from Elinor in 2007, and introduced dyslexia screening for girls in Third Form. Today, the learning support department is led by Bernie O'Neal, who organises testing, sees individual girls and advises teaching staff on how best to help them in lessons. Girls are routinely screened for dyslexia and may also be tested for processing difficulties or issues with working memory. In this way, several girls each year are aided in their learning and achieve much better outcomes than they would have been able to otherwise.

The School's efforts to ensure that each girl is able to fulfil her potential have been increasingly aided in recent years by the use of assessment and tracking data. Withington does not use the Standard Assessment Test system that obtains in state schools, but, throughout the Junior School, each girl's progress, strengths and areas for development are monitored closely. On

Experiments in the 1950s and the 2000s.

entry into Third Form, every pupil completes an assessment as part of the Middle Years Information System of tracking organised by the rather Orwellian-sounding but entirely benign Centre for Evaluation and Monitoring at the University of Durham. The results of this assessment, though not infallible, provide a basic indication of each pupil's learning strengths and weaknesses. This information helps teachers understand which aspects of academic work come naturally to each particular girl, and those where she may need to work a little more or require extra support.

This data also provides a benchmark for measuring each girl's performance in academic work, with a view to ensuring that teachers are aware not only of the highest achievers, but, more importantly, those who are making the most of their natural ability. In other words, it helps the School know who is putting in most effort and not just who is naturally most academically gifted. Notwithstanding Withington's reputation as an "academic hothouse" among those who usually do not actually know the School, its ethos is in fact that any grade a pupil achieves is counted a success if it is the best she can do, not just if it is one of the highest grades possible.

In an effort to reinforce this principle, in September 2012 the School began to publish half-termly progress grades, for attainment, attitude and organisation. The attainment grade is a measure of the standard of work each pupil has produced, but the emphasis is placed more on the other two grades: the organisation grade records whether work has been completed on time and whether the pupil has arrived at lessons punctually and well-prepared; the attitude grade is a measure of the pupil's approach to learning, her enthusiasm and participation in lessons and whether she is making the most of her individual talents.

Changes to assessment and reporting at WGS constitute just one aspect of the continuing improvement over time. The Founders envisaged that "The School should remain small, to allow for the individual development of each girl." One of

Science at Withington

In 1890 the Founders stated that "all girls should be taught the natural sciences, as it constitutes excellent intellectual training". This was far-sighted and unusual thinking for the time, since there were very few female role models, but it reflected the fact that society was changing. Indeed Manchester and other universities, including Oxford and Cambridge, had started to admit women students, albeit often on a different footing from men. The Founders also mentioned their desire for their daughters to receive a similar standard of education to their sons, a revolutionary aim at the time, though one which would appear a very modest aspiration to a present-day Withingtonian.

It is a credit to the School that it has always moved with the times, and science education has developed along with everything else. A series of Headmistresses have led investment in excellent facilities and these days lessons are taught in light, airy laboratories, rather different from the more traditional laboratories I saw when I was appointed in 1982. However, I am pleased to say that the chemistry labs still possess that distinct aroma of chemistry, so not everything changes. Since the 1980s the three sciences have been given parity in the curriculum, and all girls study them up to the age of 16, leading either to three science GCSEs or to the Double Award. The School has long had a strong tradition of science in the Sixth Form, and science A-levels are hugely popular. I can remember, during one of our inspections, the science inspector asking an Upper Fifth pupil why she thought so many girls chose to take subjects usually more popular in boys' schools. I was pleased to see that the girl, though desperate to please, could not see the point of the question – girls chose to study science because they wanted to, with no thought of gender profiling. It was as simple as that; we have come a long way since the 1890s.

I have always felt that science teachers have an advantage over teachers of other disciplines, although I suspect I am somewhat biased; after all, we can entertain with bangs and flashes, reveal the wonders of the human body or wrestle with the magnitude of the universe. But the enthusiasm has been mutual, and girls have wanted to be involved beyond the narrow confines of the curriculum. In recent years students have travelled to CERN (the European Organisation for Nuclear Research in Geneva), taken part in numerous competitions (winning quite a few), done summer research projects at the University, given public presentations and helped to communicate their love of the subject by running Junior Scientific Society and helping with SHINE, a Saturday morning club for local primary school pupils.

Of course Withington has produced young women who have excelled in their particular scientific field, but I think the School should be especially proud of its ethos that science is for all.

What will the next 125 years bring?

Jillyan Ross

CHAPTER FIVE • ACADEMIC LIFE

the features of Withington most positively remarked upon by visitors is that its small size allows just such individual knowledge and support of girls. While the School has remained true to that ideal, several programmes of limited expansion over the years have impacted on academic life.

Under Mrs Kenyon's headship, WGS expanded from two Forms per year group to three, not least to allow lower numbers of pupils in each class. Twenty-five years ago, 30 or more pupils in a class was not unusual; today, the average Form in the Senior School contains 25 pupils. The original Forms had the notations X and Y, after the axes of a graph. It would have been logical to call the new Form "Z", after the third axis of a three-dimensional graph, but Mrs Kenyon thought this might have undesirable connotations and so the new notation became, and still is, W, X and Y.

This expansion in itself did not affect the academic life of the School. It did, however, mean that timetabling became a more difficult task for Jillyan Farrell (now Ross), as classrooms and laboratories became subject to a 50 per cent increase in use. One solution was to change the timetable from the original seven-period day to an eight-period day. Under the old system, one lesson each day had to be a single period rather than a double. Science lessons in particular were not suited to the shorter time allocation. It also meant that laboratories tended to be unused for one period each day, and could be used much more efficiently if there were four double periods each day.

In parallel, the building continued to be modified and expanded, including major programmes after the fire of 2003 and the building of the new wing, which opened in 2009. Each building programme provided more space for classrooms and offices, meaning that increasingly departmental "suiting", with each subject located in a particular area of the School, became the norm. In the past, lessons took place wherever a suitable room could be timetabled, but with the increased flexibility, academic departments were able to take more ownership of particular rooms and the corridor space outside them. This

TOWARDS THE LIGHT: A PORTRAIT OF WITHINGTON GIRLS' SCHOOL

How computers have evolved ... the 1980s and 2014.

allowed them to put up more displays, making the whole building a much more stimulating and attractive place to learn.

It also meant that departmental staff had much more opportunity to work together in the same space. Jillyan Farrell remembers watching departments become more cohesive as a result, and this in turn enabled the development of the Head of Department role. In the past, a Head of Department might simply have been the most senior or longest-serving teacher of a given subject, but the role has become central to the academic life of the School and today they take a lead on teaching and learning, assessment policy and practice, planning the curriculum and management of resources to ensure the continued success of the School.

Many of these departmental developments led not only to changes to the delivery of the curriculum, but also to the subjects taught. WGS has always taken great care to ensure that the curriculum remains relevant and stimulating for the girls, preparing them for the challenges they will face in their future lives. Most recently, Dr Lorraine Earps, who was Director of Studies 2010–2013, led a wide-ranging curriculum review which explored the skills, approaches and knowledge the girls need at the start of the 21st century.

In the 1990s, Jill Bowie pioneered the teaching of psychology and, later, Tony Boyd introduced politics; both subjects were, and still are, offered to girls as A-level options. In 2003, Spanish became a further choice of modern foreign language for girls at GCSE level; previously, both French and Latin had been compulsory and German was offered in Lower Fifth Form. From 2012 onwards, girls entering Third Form have, in addition to Latin, had a free choice of two out of three modern foreign languages (French, German and Spanish), with at least one of these to be studied up to GCSE level. Economics at A-level was introduced with the appointment of Stephen Boddy in 2006 (assisted, to the extent that her

CHAPTER FIVE • ACADEMIC LIFE

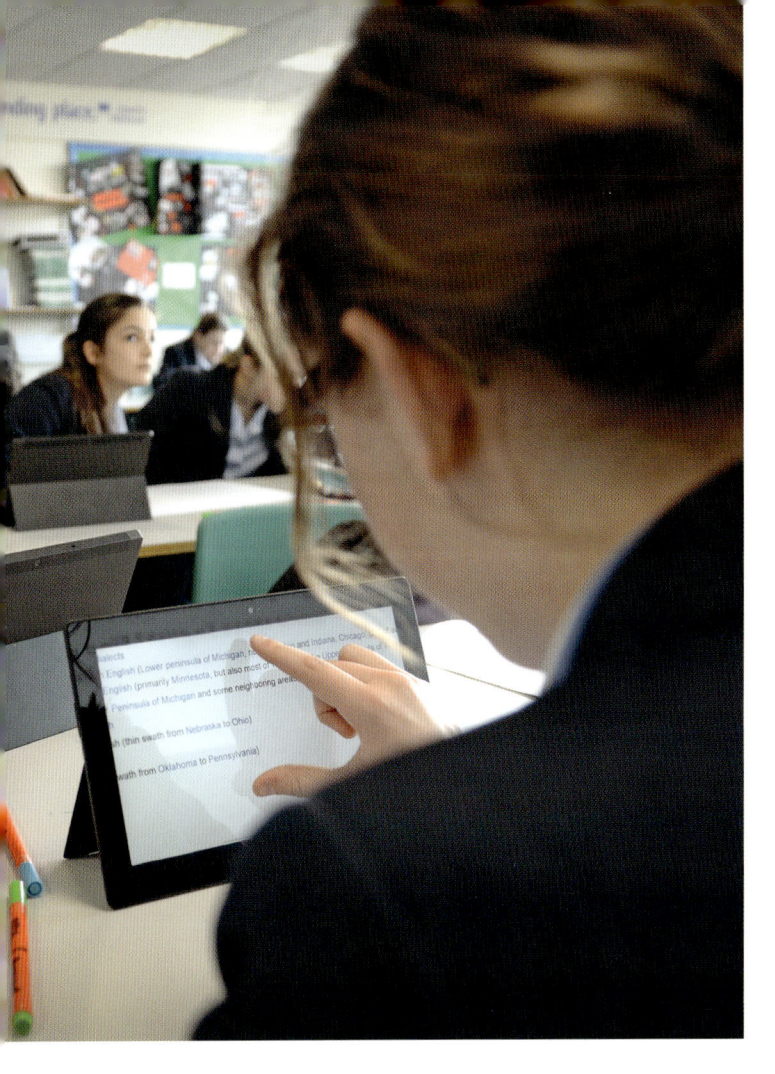

time allows, by Mrs Marks from 2012 onwards). Philosophy replaced religious studies A-level in 2012, with GCSE PE again becoming an option at the same time, and GCSE computer science began its first cycle of teaching in September 2014. In Sixth Form studies, the timetable has always been constructed around girls' requests and interests rather than pre-determined structures.

Within departments, new qualifications have recently been offered, such as the move to International GCSE courses in English, maths, French, Spanish and the sciences. It is a measure of the School's commitment to academic rigour and the best interests of its pupils that it has chosen to follow these more demanding courses irrespective of their inclusion in national league tables.

No survey of academic life over the last 25 years would be complete without mention of the most portentous development of all: the rise of the computer and the Internet. ICT was introduced to WGS by Joan Heneghan and Judy Anstice. Two of WGS's physics teachers, Ruth Lindsay-Dunn and Jasmine Renold, also taught ICT after Ruth put in a bid for a PC for the physics department. At the time, the School had one room with 16 computers, which the girls shared in pairs; there was no Internet, as it was not yet available to schools.

By 1996, Withington was connected to the World Wide Web via a single computer with a 14KB modem. There was to be no Google until two years later. Miss Renold's brother joined as ICT technician and wrote some computer code that collected and delivered emails for staff and girls once a day. It was the first instance of online communication at WGS, and soon became very popular.

More computers were added and connected to the Internet, all housed in two new computer rooms. At the turn of the millennium Mrs Kenyon had the foresight to have the whole school cabled into one big network. There is now at least one computer and a digital projector in every classroom, with 350 PCs in total around the School. WiFi, which was only introduced when Mr Lockett became Network Manager in 2009, is now ubiquitous, and is set to expand in order to enable the use of mobile technologies in classrooms throughout the School. As this happens, the nature of education itself, and not just academic life at Withington, will be transformed. Pupils will have immediate access to more information than they can possibly use, all on a small screen at their desk. The possibilities for learning are endless.

With technological changes taking place at such a pace, academic life at WGS is surely set to change rapidly. But these new modes of learning and accessing information are just new tools to add to those we have always used at Withington in pursuit of the Founders' timeless aim: "The general aim of the School will be to develop the faculties, both intellectual and physical, of the pupils, so as to enable them to continue their own education after they have left school, and to prepare them for the work of life." This preparation is explored further in Part 3.

Chapter Six

CREATIVE LIFE

> "… at Withington we are responding to the need to educate our young people for a 'post-industrial' world – one in which innovation and creativity are at a premium."
>
> – MRS SUE MARKS, HEADMISTRESS, HEAD'S LINES, WGS BULLETIN, OCTOBER 2012

MUSIC

"Vivat academia! Vivant professores! Vivat membrum quodlibet, Vivant membra quaelibet, Semper sint in flore."

– "GAUDEAMUS"

I am immensely proud to be Director of Music at Withington. Composing this piece, in collaboration with all the predecessors, colleagues and pupils who contributed memories, was hugely enjoyable – and made me even prouder. It is clear some things have never changed over the years. There is never a dull moment here, always a sense of business and purpose and a pride in work among girls and staff alike.

Until the early 1960s there was one music teacher, Miss McCardell, and school music comprised class singing lessons, one choir, and private piano lessons as an extra. There was also a rudimentary orchestra. Curriculum music developed with Miss Boswell's arrival in 1962 and the introduction of GCE music. In 1964 Miss Jean Fielden replaced Miss Boswell, and music reached the Sixth Form. Instrumental teaching grew

Right: Miss McCardell at the piano in 1956.

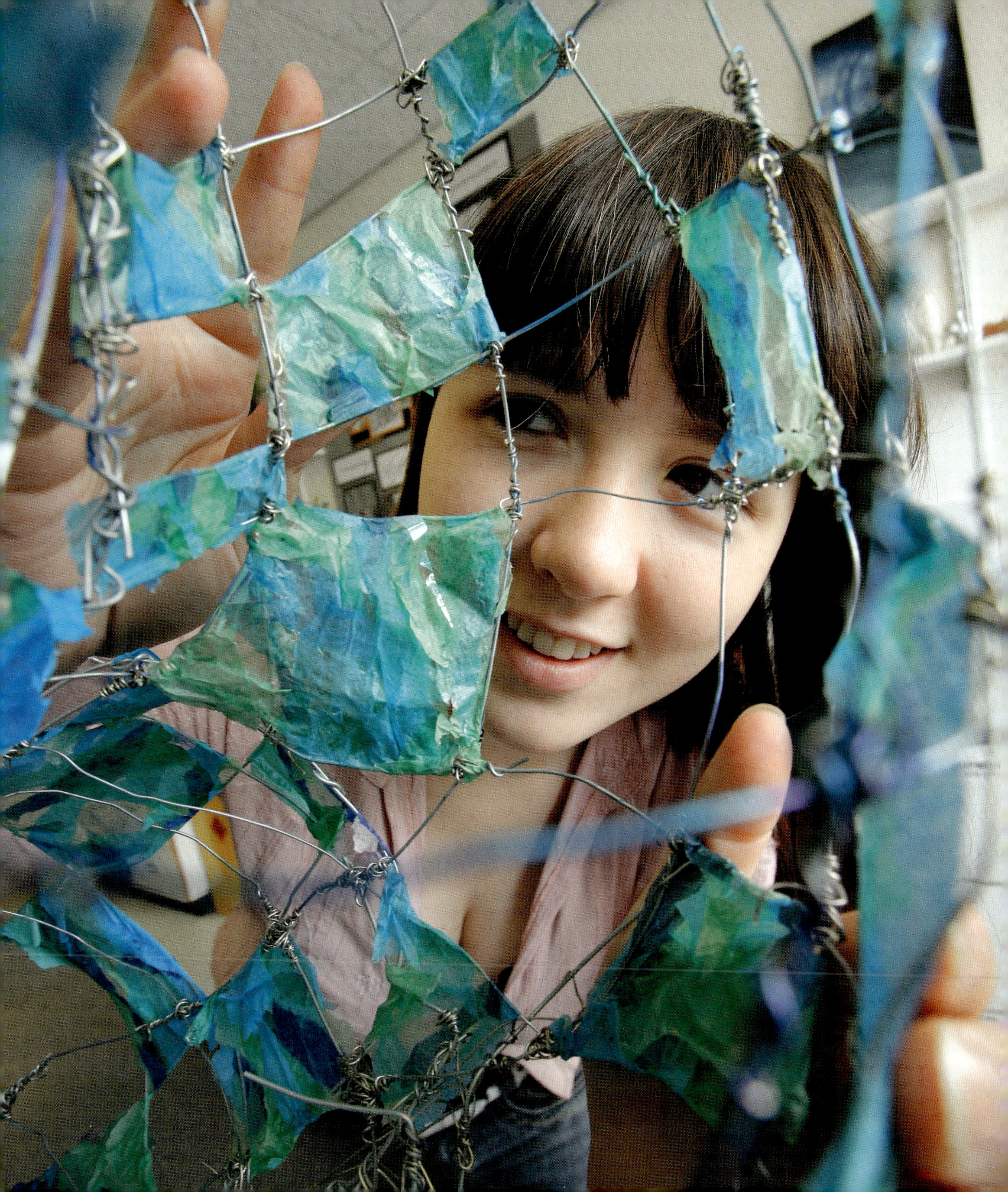

and increasing numbers of peripatetics made a full Senior Orchestra possible, a Junior Orchestra providing an excellent training ground. In 1968 Christine Manning succeeded Miss McCardell and soon formed the popular Wind Band. Accommodation for all this activity was a logistical challenge; lessons took place wherever there was space, including the main hall and even a kitchen.

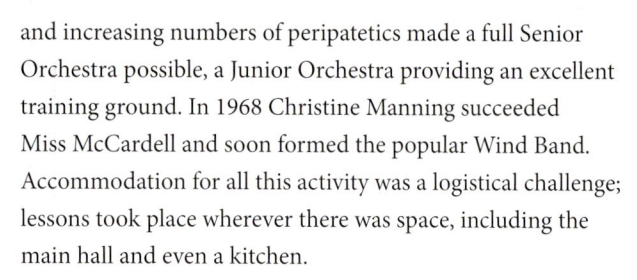

Then the Arts Centre was built. Officially opened by Judith and Sandra Chalmers in 1982, it afforded ample room for instrumental lessons, storage, and of course rehearsals, concerts and shows. This fantastic performance venue was made for music and drama to join forces. First, in 1988, came Benjamin Britten's *Noye's Fludde*, a whole-school production in every sense, showing Withington at its best. As Jean Fielden says, "The shape of the hall was perfect – the gallery above the stage was ideal for the appearance of 'God' and then became the Ark. One cast member has since become a world famous opera singer – Christine Rice was our Mrs Noah."

To me, being part of a school show is the opportunity of a lifetime, bringing challenges and rewards, new friends, teams and experiences, tests of patience and perseverance. *Noye's Fludde* was the first of many joint music and drama productions: *Guys and Dolls, Jesus Christ Superstar, My Fair Lady, The Wiz* and my first WGS musical, 2011's *Joseph*, with its cast of over a hundred girls. Our music students also frequently compose incidental music for drama productions, notably *The First Pirate Queen* (written by playwright Charlotte Keatley after workshops with the girls to develop their ideas), which had its world premiere in the Arts Centre in November 2005.

By the 1980s curricular music was firmly established and extra-curricular ensembles were thriving. Word spread, and Withington's musicians were asked to perform at numerous concerts outside school. This included a performance at the Royal Northern College of Music (RNCM), with our singers in the highest gallery of the College's concert hall dovetailing meticulously with its own choir below.

CHAPTER SIX • CREATIVE LIFE

Christine Rice

Christine Rice is recognised as one of the leading mezzo-sopranos of her generation. In her final year at Withington, the School put on an unusual choice for a student production, and *Noye's Fludde* was to be Christine's first opera of many. Christine took piano and violin lessons and participated in both the Manchester Youth Orchestra and Theatre throughout her childhood and teenage years. From school, Christine remembers best her maths teacher, Mrs Ford, and her passionate and clear revelation of the beauty and simplicity of numbers. Christine went on to study physics at Oxford then, after a late "gap year" at the RNCM, decided on a career in singing. Nowadays she regularly performs at major opera houses all over Europe and the USA but still has fond memories of Manchester and, as an avid and regular spectator at the Royal Exchange Theatre, of its rich cultural life. Although operas can take years to come together, from the initial enquiry about whether she is interested in a role to rehearsals and finally performances, Christine says she loves it all. She tries however to keep the travelling, which can be extensive, to a minimum whenever possible. Christine chose *The Concise Oxford Companion to English Literature* for her Founders' Day presentation, and says of her school days:

I was a somewhat lacklustre violinist as a teenager and lurked at the back of the seconds in orchestra, but, by the Sixth Form, I was treated to an unforgettable musical experience, that of appearing in Noye's Fludde. *If I remember correctly it was also my first introduction to the genius of Benjamin Britten. What a uniquely ambitious school Withington is!*

Christine returned to the School on two occasions: in 2001, when she sang excerpts from *Carmen* with the Senior Choir and Orchestra, and again in 2009, when she performed the aria "O Don Fatale" from Verdi's opera *Don Carlo*.

Emma Willan and Gilly Sargent

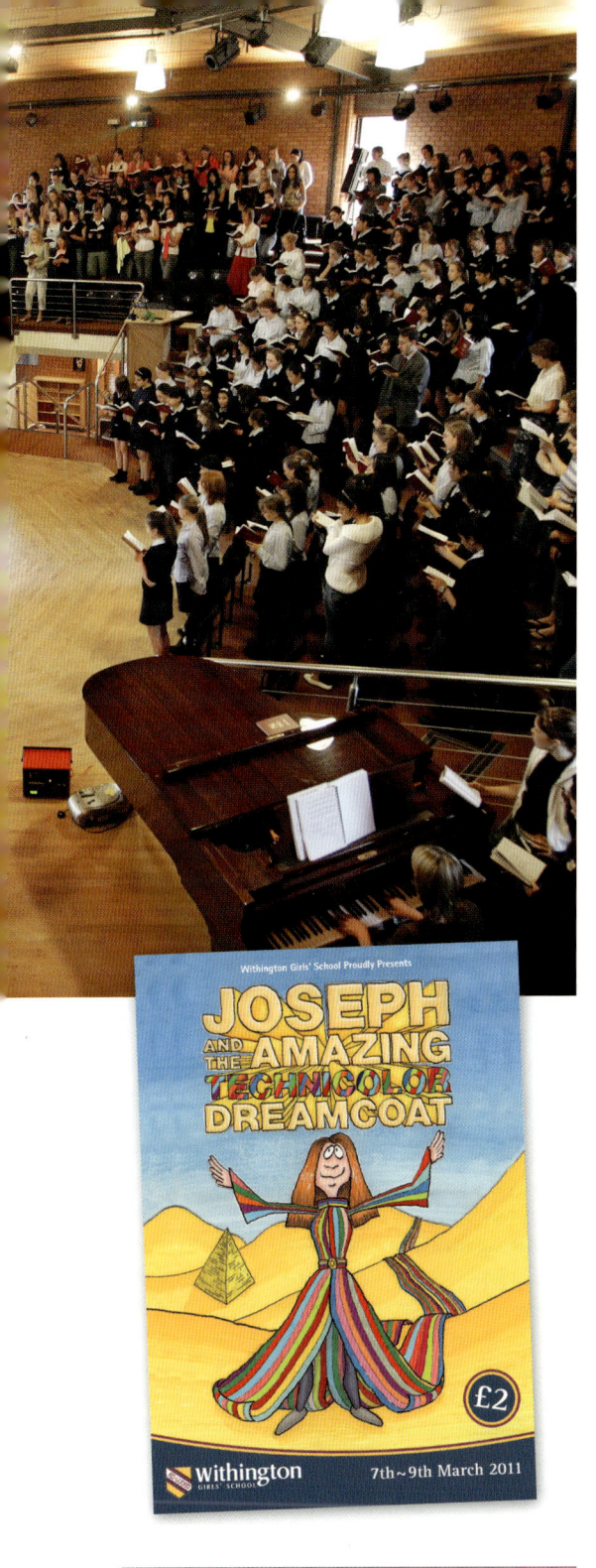

Clockwise from top left: music staff past and present meet to pool memories for this chapter; the Arts Centre; advertising Joseph; *Judith and Sandra Chalmers open the Arts Centre in 1982.*

Sasha Johnson Manning

Sasha Johnson Manning – former pupil, daughter of Christine Manning and highly accomplished composer – has had a long and close association with the School. I was delighted when she became a Governor: with her interest in making links and developing the girls' musical experience to the full, she epitomises the Withington spirit. Sasha composed "O Light Invisible", a wonderful piece performed at Founders' Day and the Centenary celebrations in 1990 and the first of many commissions. Her beautiful Millenium anthem, "Endless Days", was performed by the Senior Choir at the first Founders' Day at the Bridgewater Hall. It was a joy to have Sasha and her expertise on board again for Founders' Day 2010 and the girls' all-important annual performance, this time featuring her choral arrangement of Samuel Barber's "Adagio for Strings" ("Nigra sum sed Formosa") and her song "Go tell someone" (also recorded for Radio 4's *Sunday Worship*). Sasha asked the Junior School Choir to join the premiere performance of her acclaimed Manchester Carols at the Royal Northern College of Music in 2007, and they were invited back for a second performance at Christmas 2008. Sasha came on tour with us to Italy in 2011 and our rehearsals of her own "Melodica" will remain a memory of a lifetime.

Gilly Sargent

Sasha remembers her time at the School very fondly. The Senior Choir made a great impression on her: she describes their singing as "so beautiful and heavenly" and she loved listening and being part of it. Leaving Withington was a "huge wrench" after "the loving security" of the School. She remembers particularly vividly a power cut when she was allowed to wear her own clothes to school. Candles had been lit and placed all around the building, giving a magical feel. The hymn that morning had the line "Let there be light" at the end of every verse, much to the hilarity of Sasha and the rest of the School, and it is still her favourite hymn to this day. Sasha works with the classics as well as the music department at WGS, helping Latin students. She also travels widely: her hymn "Revelation in Exile", written for the choir of St Martin-in-the-Fields, was performed in the US President's Church in Washington, close to the White House.

Ella Pennington

On Jean's retirement in 1988, Chris Holmes, an accomplished jazz musician, became Musical Director. Chris and Christine took the show on the road, and a wonderful performance in the Sainsbury's Choir of the Year competition earned the choir second place. In School, the many prestigious concerts included *A Baroque Evening* with both WGS and MGS musicians, and of course the Centenary production *Northern Lights*.

In 1992 Christine retired and Alison Bailey joined the team. Chris's jazz group was invited to perform at the Girls' Schools Association's conference at the Midland Hotel during Mrs Kenyon's presidency of the GSA in 1993, and the same year, in contrast, a lovely evening of concertos for Valentine's Day exemplified the very high standard of instrumental playing. Soloist Anna Wolstenholme went on to reach the woodwind finals of the Young Musician of the Year competition. Musical success meant growing links with the media and performances at major events and recordings, including appearances for the Senior Choir in *My Favourite Hymns* (Granada TV), James MacMillan's *Magnificat* (for Radio 3) and *Songs of Praise* with Aled Jones at the Bridgewater Hall.

The year 2002 brought both new music classrooms in the Margaret Kenyon Wing, which made an amazing difference

CHAPTER SIX • CREATIVE LIFE

L to R: the Music Summer School; a School orchestra.

to lessons, and a new Director, Andrew Dean. Andrew's first two major tasks were to equip the rooms with IT facilities, keyboards and the music programme Sibelius for examination classes, and to organise a choir tour to Italy, including a performance at the Basilica di San Marco. Both were successfully achieved, paving the way for future development.

Meanwhile Alison, an accomplished composer and orchestrator, was working on enabling more young people from the local community to take part in music-making at Withington. The first Music Summer School, directed by instrumental teachers Tim Chatterton and Becca Thompson, took place in 2004 and was open to eight- to 18-year-olds, including those with learning disabilities and hearing impairments. Workshops included dance, Dalcroze eurythmics, Urban Strawberry Lunch (making music from junk), folk and gospel singing, gamelan steel pans, MC skills and beat boxing. The Summer School ran hugely successfully until 2010, with many participants going on to Conservatoires, Chetham's School of Music and Oxbridge. To quote one parent: "Without the course my child would never have begun to play an instrument. It was the most formative event in their childhood and where they gained the experience to enhance their understanding of what music can be … how it connects to creativity … it was a total inspiration to them."

At the same time a joint project with the Northern Chamber Orchestra (NCO), sponsored by the Department for Education, was aiming to build bridges between the state and independent sectors, widening educational opportunities and sharing best practice. GCSE groups from WGS and Trinity Church of England (C of E) High School worked with the NCO, composing for its musicians and learning about their work, culminating in a fantastic performance at the RNCM in summer 2005.

At the end of this term both Andrew and Alison retired and the baton in this musical relay passed to me and my assistant Amy Holland. Our first task was to keep all the plates spinning. Work with the NCO and Trinity C of E High School progressed, including two performances of solo concertos, accompanied by the Orchestra, in 2006 and 2008 (one of the soloist performers was Imogen Lewis Holland, who, aged sixteen, reached the regional finals of Young Musician of the Year). Links remain strong to this day: many of our instrumental staff regularly perform with the NCO, and we continue to benefit from their composition expertise in workshops for our GCSE and A-level groups.

One of the joys of Withington is its ability to combine the new with the old – particularly evident at Christmas. The School's annual Carol Service has long taken place at St Ann's, with an *a cappella* rehearsal outside the church now enjoyed by shoppers at the German Markets, and a hasty Christmas dinner for the Senior Choir beforehand. Since 2005, we have taken part in the Tree of Lights service at Manchester Cathedral in aid of St Ann's Hospice: a most poignant occasion, with the Cathedral lit up by candles in memory of those loved and lost. The Senior Orchestra and Senior Choir perform too at the Christmas party for local senior citizens (see Chapter 9) accompanied by dancing trees, Christmas puddings and stars – and a new tradition. Mrs Marks' singalong Golden Oldies have included wonderful renditions of "Que Sera Sera" and "Moon River" – it must be the Welsh blood in her! Finally the Music Festival, originally a tribute concert to Miss McCardell, is also now part of the end-of-year celebrations, held biennially in rotation with Spoken English.

Such links with the community have always been vitally important to the music department and the School as a whole, and we have also contributed to local royal and sporting occasions. Chris recalls organising music for outdoor Golden Jubilee celebrations with many a clothes peg coming to the rescue, while simultaneously preparing a performance to celebrate the Commonwealth Games held in Manchester in 2002. And I arranged "Sing", composed by Gary Barlow and Andrew Lloyd Webber for the Diamond Jubilee celebrations in 2012, as a fanfare for the opening of our Olympic Games celebrations on Citizenship Day that same exciting year.

Music has always been closely linked with fundraising both in and out of school. The department has received unfailing support over the years from the PTA – including the purchase of the grand piano to mark the Centenary, two upright pianos for the practice rooms and a lever harp, as well as support for the P Bones Brass Project – and has always been keen to reciprocate

CHAPTER SIX • CREATIVE LIFE

Clockwise from left: Mrs Marks leads the singing and trees dance at the Christmas party; massed ukuleles.

Where are Music Alumnae Now?

Imogen Lewis Holland is Artist Manager to Sir Simon Rattle at Askonas Holt. She remembers constant support, positivity and excellent teaching from "inspirational" staff, and plenty of opportunities to perform.

Sarah Holmes is studying at York St John University, with hopes of becoming a head of Junior School music. Music "helped me find my place in the Withington community" – as well as being "a lot of fun".

Tori Longdon is a Choral Director, Artistic Director and Animateur in London with groups including the National Youth Choir: "terms flew by, one whirling week of music groups after another!"

Clare Owens is teaching classics at Cheadle Hulme School – still playing the flute and piano and a member of several choirs, with "very fond memories" of music at WGS and the encouragement of staff.

Susan Wollenberg is Professor of Music at Oxford University. She remembers "lots of different musical opportunities" and (with a smile) a school report wondering if she was "spending too much time on her music"!

with music at Spring Fairs and PTA Balls. In 2010, a 12-hour Musathon was planned to raise money for the PTA who, following the earthquake in Haiti, kindly agreed that the money raised should go to the disaster appeal. Pupils and staff gave 15-minute performances over a 12-hour period, raising £2,000.

And so to the present! The plates are still spinning and new projects have joined existing. We now have, courtesy of the Annual Fund, a concert pedal harp to go with the lever harp bought by the PTA, meaning Withington boasts one of the biggest school harp departments in the north-west. All the Juniors now learn an instrument within the curriculum – 90 ukuleles en masse is a sight to behold! Both music classrooms are equipped with the latest version of Sibelius as well as the necessary computers and keyboards, and recording facilities

TOWARDS THE LIGHT: A PORTRAIT OF WITHINGTON GIRLS' SCHOOL

The Choir in Barcelona (left); and the School is alive with The Sound of Music *in 2014.*

are in the pipeline. The uptake in music means we now have two GCSE groups, and 19 different extra-curricular activities (encompassing theory, performance and composition) take place each week, with on average two external performances every half term. Many girls have been offered places in the Hallé's Youth Orchestra, Youth Choir and Children's Choir. There has been considerable success at university level too, with a number of girls winning music scholarships to Oxbridge.

Music department trips have included a 2007 Choir tour to Barcelona and a return visit to Italy and the Basilica di San Marco, where we sang at Mass, in 2011. As I write, music and drama are planning our latest whole-school production – *The Sound of Music* – and a tour to Austria to see where it all happened.

"Towards the Light" is such an apt phrase for the music department at Withington. As society changes, so music evolves and searches for new directions. The ability and the conviction of the girls will always take us towards the light, and I am proud to be part of the process and to be carrying the baton right now.

Gilly Sargent

CHAPTER SIX • CREATIVE LIFE

91

TOWARDS THE LIGHT: A PORTRAIT OF WITHINGTON GIRLS' SCHOOL

DRAMA

"There are some paths, in art as in life, where just the angels consent to tread … and we are on the side of the angels."

– FROM PROFESSOR HERFORD'S REVIEW OF *A JACOBEAN MASQUE* AT WITHINGTON, PUBLISHED IN THE *MANCHESTER GUARDIAN* 1912

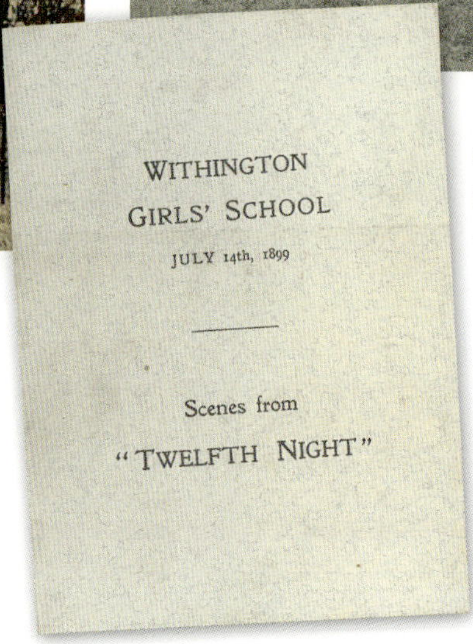

It seems that even as far back as 1912, Withington pupils and staff were making theatre that challenged and inspired audiences. The Jacobean Masque referred to above had not been performed since the 17th century until a WGS company obtained the piece and performed it with "much courage, devotion … and considerable resources".

Courage, devotion and considerable resources. I'd say that's drama at Withington in a nutshell. Courage, of course, permeates the history of the School itself as well as the story of drama within it. How much courage did it take for our Founders to establish a school for girls at a time when prevailing beliefs suggested that education of women was detrimental not only to women themselves but to society as a whole? And once this school had begun, how much courage has it taken for successive members of the School to stand up within the community, take the stage and speak to their audiences? How much courage does it still take?

Research by Miss Joyce Boucher into the history of drama at the School, published in the *Celebration of the first hundred years*, recounts many individual and collective acts of courage and vision, from the "scenes from" that characterised the very early days of performance at the School to the Centenary production of *Northern Lights* in the Arts Centre in 1990. I enter this story

92

CHAPTER SIX • CREATIVE LIFE

Shakespeare at Withington. Left: Twelfth Night, *1899; above,* Two Gentlemen of Verona, *1950.*

Joyce Hytner OBE

Joyce Hytner has always had a passion for drama. After leaving Withington, that passion led to a career which included the position of Head of Development at the Royal Court Theatre and a consultancy with Granada Television. Joyce is currently Chairman of Act IV, the company she set up several years ago, which is dedicated to supporting the arts. Joyce remains active and influential in the theatre; she sits on the boards of the Old Vic, the Royal Court and Criterion Theatres, the Manchester International Festival and The Charterhouse. She has dedicated her life to the dramatic arts and has been instrumental in fundraising for this cause, previously being a trustee of the Lowry in Salford, as well as both LAMDA and the Royal Northern College of Music; she was a trustee of St Paul's Cathedral Foundation until 2012. Joyce has also lent her support and fundraising expertise to the WGS Bursary Appeal, hosting an exclusive fundraising film screening for Alumnae in London, and to the major outdoor production of *Romeo and Juliet* put on by WGS and other schools. She has passed on her passion for drama to her son, Sir Nicholas Hytner, Director of the National Theatre from 2003 to 2015.

Rosie Martland

for the first time in 1985 as a pupil, playing the title role in *The Mikado* – a Junior School production directed by Monica Hastings in the recently constructed Arts Centre – determined to play the part with all the courage and devotion my ten-year-old self could muster. In 2001, an act of courage and vision from Mrs Pickering established drama as a department in its own right at Withington. That's where I re-enter the story, as Withington's first Head of Drama. Bringing a vision and courage of my own and happily finding it matched by the pupils who were willing then and are willing now to take a leap of faith with every project, we invented a drama department that was in one sense new and in another sense built on foundations that were as old as the School itself.

The world premiere of The First Pirate Queen *in 2005 involved aerial sequences, sword fighting and the construction of a vast pirate ship.*

While devotion to drama was pretty much at the top of the job specification for that particular role, I wasn't the first pupil or teacher to be devoted to drama at school and I certainly won't be the last. Throughout our history, members of our school have recognised the power of drama and the richness of the traditions that we share. As we play together, so we laugh and cry together. We explore possibilities, push at boundaries, and reflect on who we are and what makes us human. Joyce Boucher's researches ended with her own production of *Northern Lights*, devised after a career devoted to drama. Those who were responsible for school drama in the years between 1990 and my arrival in 2001, including Marie Green and Monica Hastings, ably assisted by staff from all areas of the School, had done so with genuine devotion to the subject, and

CHAPTER SIX • CREATIVE LIFE

Judith and Sandra Chalmers

As "proud old girls" of Withington Judith and Sandra have gone on to forge successful careers in broadcasting and the media and recognise that the education they received at WGS has stayed with them throughout their lives. Their mother, Millie Chalmers, widowed at the age of 44, was determined that the girls should receive the best education Manchester could offer. They were both 13 when they first broadcast in *BBC Children's Hour* from Manchester.

Judith Chalmers OBE

Judith is a well-known TV and radio personality. She continued to broadcast in the North Region of the BBC and Granada TV after leaving school before moving to London where she became a senior BBC TV announcer. She also presented *Come Dancing*, was a news reporter, commentated for ten years at Royal Ascot on the fashions, and on radio introduced *Two-Way Family Favourites* and *Weekend Woman's Hour*. On TV and radio she commentated at Royal and State occasions including the Queen's Silver Jubilee and the wedding of Prince Charles and Lady Diana Spencer. On ITV at Thames TV she hosted *Miss World* for five years and the travel programme *Wish You Were Here?* which ran for 30 years with an average audience of 13 million. In 2002 she was honoured at the British Travel Awards for her outstanding contribution to travel and tourism and in 2003 the British Guild of Travel Writers presented her with their Lifetime Achievement Award. She is President Emeritus of The Lady Taverners and for 20 years was Chairman of the Appeals Committee of the Women's National Cancer Control Campaign.

Sandra Chalmers

Sandra is a communications consultant whose company, Chalmers Communications, specialises in public affairs and media training. After her first *Children's Hour* play, she continued to freelance with the BBC and Granada Television while at university. Joining the BBC as a member of staff, she became Editor of *Woman's Hour* in the 1980s, and then created the BBC's Radio Publicity and Promotions department. She is regularly called upon to act as an expert contributor on over-50s issues for radio and television. Sandra believes that WGS gave her the confidence to pursue her career in broadcasting, the media and charity work. She will never forget playing Archbishop Thomas Becket in Joyce Boucher's production of *Murder in the Cathedral* and, a good few years later, leading a rousing chorus of "Gaudeamus" at the School's 100th Anniversary Dinner.

Christine Davies

the hours they spent developing drama outside the curriculum were very much a labour of love.

That devotion remains at the heart of the drama department today. Drama has finally found its way into all levels of the curriculum, and a girl with a passion for drama can now study it as a subject in its own right, with its own unique skill set, all the way from Third Form to the Upper Sixth. We can see anything from five to ten examination

Above: Trafford Tanzi, *2006; right:* The Tempest, *2008.*

performances in the studio each year, alongside a range of extra-curricular projects. All projects, be they performed as part of our curriculum or as an extension of it, are designed to capture the imagination and make our souls sing. Whether we are joining with 14 other schools across Manchester to perform the huge outdoor *Romeo and Juliet* in the MGS quadrangle or commissioning Charlotte Keatley to write a play about pirate queens, whether we are exploring love and life in intricate two-handers in the studio or putting half the School on stage in a musical epic, we are always hoping to speak directly and relevantly of ourselves and our world to our audience.

It is pretty much a law of theatre that we always want more than we have available, but we are still lucky enough to enjoy "considerable resources" at Withington. Of course the major development in recent years has been the introduction of a space in the School that is dedicated to the learning and teaching of drama. Our studio began life as a converted section of the Lesser Hall in 2001 and in 2009 was extended into the studio that we know today. Beginning with just a handful of lanterns and no sound system, we now have the technical capacity to match (and even better) studios in professional theatres. Happily, it is still purple. Had it not been for the imagination and support of Mrs Pickering it would not have existed at all.

There have been other additions in terms of resources: in 2007 we introduced the LAMDA curriculum to run alongside our curricular and extra-curricular projects, allowing girls access to specialist actor training from an early age in our LAMDA studio. We have gone from being a one-man band to a team of six, and there is a technical crew of girls trained to work on sound, lighting and stage management. Mrs Marks is now the one who decides what resources are allocated to us, but she does so with a twinkle in her eye and an appreciation that worth and value cannot be calculated by doing sums.

Of course the official accounts of our drama story tend to be a record of the end results rather than the journeys we undergo to achieve them, so a list of people, spaces and performances stretching back from this year's celebration of our 125th anniversary is only ever going to be part of the story. The impact of drama within our school is impossible to quantify, but it is nevertheless palpable at every turn. As pupils and staff challenge each other to take risks, think creatively and constantly change and develop our practice, it is never easy – and always nerve-racking – but we know that the drama we make is woven into the fabric of our school and we look forward to playing our role in the next 125 years and beyond.

And we intend to stay on the side of the angels.

Jen Baylis

ART

"The pupils' ability to be creative and original is seen in striking artwork."

– 2013 INSPECTORS

Delving through the archives and immersing myself in the recent history of creativity in Withington's art department has proved both interesting and inspiring. It has opened up new avenues and possibilities for development that I might not have discovered otherwise.

Annual departmental reports have provided the richest source of information, often written by the Head of Art but sometimes including personal accounts by girls who have experienced something quite memorable and magical on their artistic journey at Withington.

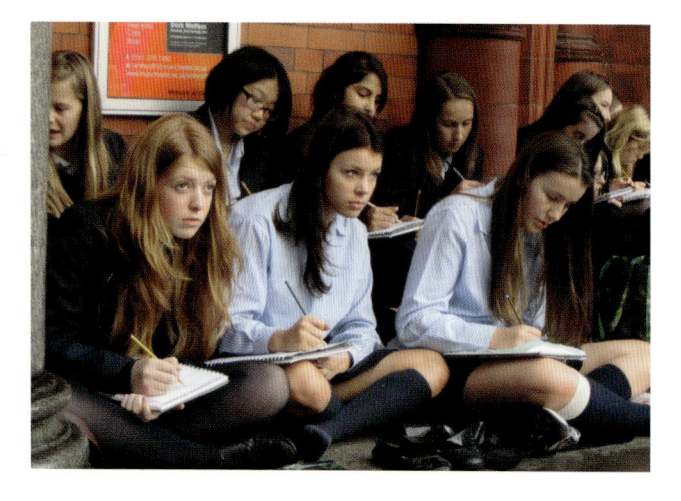

There are many parallels between the past and the way we work today, but we have advanced and improved as each year has passed. It is reassuring to see that the old faithful, tried and tested, genres of art are evident throughout the last 25 years, but the way they have been approached and developed has varied enormously. Portraiture, still-life, architecture and nature have provided, and continue to provide, a wealth of imagery and ideas for the girls and their projects. The A-level group studying architecture in 1992 who "braved the elements to spend a day sketching in Manchester, despite train delays and the monstrous drizzle" reminded me instantly of our most recent visit to the Manchester Museum. The current Lower Fifth artists worked so diligently and skilfully outside the Museum, drawing amongst the blooming allotment in the cold and windy Manchester weather.

The work of great artists such as Monet, da Vinci and van Gogh has been an important source of inspiration for our girls. There have been many trips to the National Gallery for essential first-hand research and there is nothing more breathtaking than experiencing magnificent artwork up close and personal! In 1994, works viewed by the Sixth Form in London included memorable pieces created by Leonardo da Vinci, and how can his vast body of work not continue to help us with our self-portraiture (seen in the current sketchbook work of the Upper Fourth)?

The art room in 1953 and 2013.

The Bain Collection

The School's Bain Art Collection owes its existence to a painting belonging to Mary Elspeth Bain, Headmistress 1938–1961. A colleague recalled that Miss Bain "possessed a natural eye for colour and design. … [her room] was illuminated by some attractive pictures by Anne Redpath, the Scottish artist, a friend from student days".[1] The reference to art's illuminating quality is fitting for a school whose motto still is "Towards the Light". Through Miss Bain's generosity, the School acquired the works by Redpath (1895–1965), the only woman member of the Edinburgh School of artists that revelled in bright colours and strong expressive forms.[2]

In 2006 the sale of one of Redpath's paintings allowed Withington to establish the Bain Art Collection, motivated by a wish to have on display a range of artworks to uplift and inspire all those who attend, work at or visit the School. Many of the artists of the 29 works currently in the Collection have local connections, and several are still working. All works are two-dimensional, domestic-sized pieces executed in a range of media including paint, pen, tapestry and mixed media. Several works are located in the busiest footfall area around the central staircase; others attract attention in significant locations near the careers office, in the junior wing, by the development office and on the stairway to the recently refurbished art rooms. The "hang" is made more striking and impressive by the juxtaposition of these pieces with stunning artworks produced by Withington's own students.

Many works in the Collection are landscapes. A number tend towards the realism tradition; others abstract the landscape. In Florian Foerster's *Railway Bridges, Manchester* (left), colour blocking suggests both the profile of the superstructure and a sense of spatial depth as the viewer passes under the bridge. Appropriately, a Redpath painting remains in the Headmistress's study (below). The poise of composition allied with the imaginative colour palette offers a space to reflect on reaching towards the light.

Anne Kirkham

CHAPTER SIX • CREATIVE LIFE

Extra-curricular activities are an integral part of the art, craft and design experiences at school, taking many forms and involving a wide variety of people. I was delighted to come across a 2004 photograph of an intent-looking Mr Sharples, hand-sculpting a cat during an adult ceramic class run by Diane Connell, Head of Art at the time. Girls have the opportunity to participate throughout their time at the School, and benefit from the expertise and experiences of staff who are practising artists in their own right. One pupil said of her experience of Junior Tapestry Club, "I managed to make two beautiful rugs. There are teachers there to help and it is great fun." Recently pupils have successfully created glowing withy lanterns and textural ceramic perfume bottles, and even turned their hand to book-binding. Over the years Mosaic Club has been a popular activity, and in 2012 girls and staff, along with doctors and patients at the Royal Manchester Children's Hospital, designed and created an eight-foot-high mosaic depicting a bright and colourful arching rainbow – an exciting and rewarding commission for the Hospital's Harrington Building.

Other enriching experiences have included visits by professional artists, whose wide-ranging skills and talents have benefited our whole community. In 2007 Florian Foerster

The quality of the academic education at Withington goes without saying. Looking back I particularly value the stimulus of some of the other teachers in giving us a rounded education. I couldn't do GCE art because it clashed with an academic subject, but Miss Harrison stimulated my interest in art history (which led to an MA almost 50 years later!). She trusted and encouraged three of us in the Sixth Form to paint a mural of the Seven Ages of Man along the corridor outside the art room.

– DIANA WOOLDRIDGE (HALL) (1965)

An adult ceramic class.

101

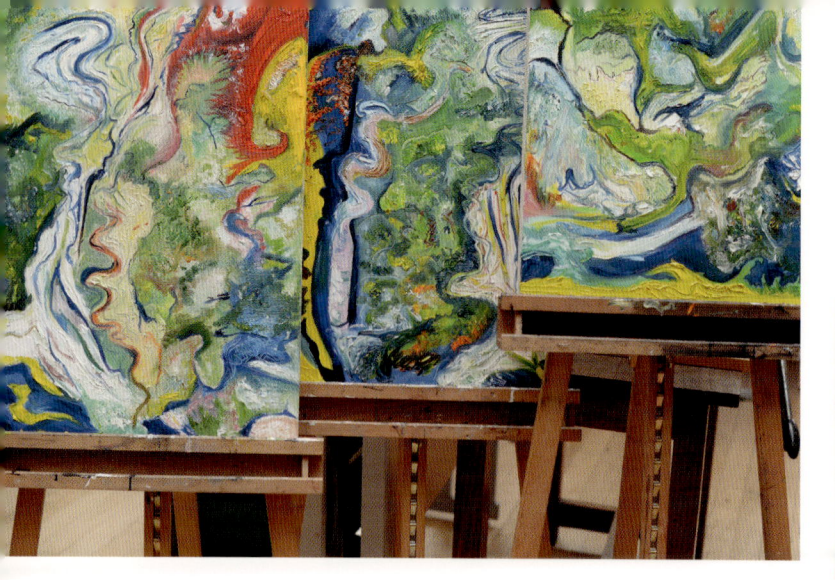

shared his practice with the GCSE and A-level artists and two pieces of his work form part of our Bain Art Collection. During 2010, Charlotte Newson delivered a memorable talk and a unique practical workshop to girls, parents and staff as part of her *Women Like You* exhibition at Manchester Art Gallery. Some girls were delighted to see their work displayed at the gallery in the form of digital artwork as part of a short film.

The summer break has also proved a fruitful time for art activities. In the early 2000s, under special government funding, a relationship was forged between our art department and that of Whalley Range High School for Girls. Between us we organised a summer school focusing on art, craft and design activities. This has now developed into an annual event open to the whole Withington community. The art summer workshops have been a huge success for girls, boys and staff alike, instigating amongst other things the creation of monstrous giant octopuses, recycled robots and insect-inspired millinery.

Display of the girls' creative endeavours through exhibition has long been an important feature of the School's calendar. It is a deserved celebration and recognition of their hard work and talents, and their achievements at GCSE and A-level. Venues in School have included the undercroft, the entrance area and foyer, the Sixth Form common room, and the newly refurbished and beautifully lit art studios.

Outside School, exhibition venues have included the Portico Library and the Lowry Art Gallery, and a permanent collection of breathtaking vista paintings has now joined the mosaic to light up the Harrington Building at the Royal Manchester Children's Hospital.

The department's facilities have evolved and improved over time. But it was pleasing to stumble across an old black-and-white photograph of a class of girls sitting in a very recognisable large art room, focused intently on a still-life arrangement – and there is certainly a case to be made for the more traditional methods of drawing! Between the summers

CHAPTER SIX • CREATIVE LIFE

of 1992 and 1993, one of my predecessors, Diane Connell, was dreaming of her new, more spacious art studio with adjoining pottery studio: "We secretly thought gremlins had been at work puffing dust through the holes in the walls between us and the new building work … net curtains diffuse the bright sunlight that used to stream in through the windows". I also dreamt of a new art studio whilst on my maternity leave, 20 years later in the summer of 2012, and how lucky I was to return in 2013 to find that the whole department had been refurbished to meet the needs of the growing numbers of Withington art students and the requirements of the contemporary art world.

I am delighted that some of our immensely talented girls decide to further their study in the art field after leaving Withington, going on to study architecture at degree level or pursue art foundation courses. Of course we are proud that Sarah Burton, Creative Director of Alexander McQueen and designer of Catherine Middleton's wedding dress, is an Alumna; and there are many other examples of highly successful careers that have blossomed from seeds carefully and creatively nurtured within our art department. To give just two recent examples – Kamilla Kocialkowski, who left in 2005, is a freelance journalist and art critic in London, and has worked on both the Royal Academy and *Tate Etc.* magazines. Harriet Cooper (who also left in 2005) is on the curating team at the world-renowned Yorkshire Sculpture Park. Both are amazing career achievements in such a short space of time. I am also proud that our girls are going on to the very best universities, such as Central Saint Martins and the Slade School of Fine Art. This is testament to their outstanding ideas and abilities and I very much look forward to following their careers into the future.

Ruth Fildes

Sarah Burton OBE

Sarah Burton was born in Macclesfield, Cheshire. After attending WGS from the age of seven, she completed a foundation course at Manchester Polytechnic. She went on to study Print Fashion at Central Saint Martins College in London, at the suggestion of one of her "most inspiring" teachers at Withington, Mrs Diane Connell. After graduating in 1997, Sarah returned to the Alexander McQueen office where she had worked as an intern the previous year. She was appointed head of womenswear in 2000, and, following Alexander McQueen's death in February 2010, became creative director in May the same year. After months of speculation before the royal wedding in 2011, it was revealed on the day that Sarah had created the gown worn by Catherine Middleton for her marriage to Prince William. Sarah lives in St John's Wood, London, with her photographer husband, David Burton. She has received critical acclaim for her collections at McQueen, and in 2012 was named in *Time 100*, an annual list of the 100 most influential people in the world. In 2011 she was named Designer of the Year at the British Fashion Awards, and in 2012 received the OBE for her services to the British fashion industry.

Isabella Risino

Chapter Seven

SPORTING LIFE

Mary Rawsthorn

"The daily playing of games for the last hour each morning has always been a noteworthy feature in the life of the School. Much of the freshness and vitality of the girls is no doubt due to this wise arrangement."

– 1924 INSPECTORS

In 1878 Madame Bergman-Osterberg was employed by the London School Board to teach Swedish gymnastics: a defining moment in girls' physical education in England. In order to spread her teaching methods throughout the country she founded Dartford College of Physical Education, one of whose pupils, Margaret Stansfeld, went on to found Bedford College of Physical Education. Miss Stansfeld taught future Withington Headmistress Miss Grant, who, when the new gymnasium was opened in 1934, asked her former games teacher to perform the official ceremony. I am thrilled by this impressive historical link.

Games and gymnastics were soon established as the base for physical education in girls' schools and this has always been the Withington way. The 1904 *Newsletter* reports that former pupil Theodora Steinhal had completed her training at Anstey as a teacher of Swedish educational and medicinal gymnastics, while Esther Loveday had gone to Stockholm to train in Swedish drill at the National Institute. From her time at the School in the 1940s, Morag McCaig remembers hockey, lacrosse, netball, cricket, tennis and especially "Pirates". She also referred fondly to her games mistress, Miss Corfe.

Over the years WGS has tried a range of activities from archery to Zumba, responding to current trends, the girls' enthusiasms, teachers' expertise and the National Curriculum. All pupils have had a well-rounded experience in lessons, with generous timetabling and continuing provision of good facilities – starting with a large on-the-spot games field, thanks to Founder Emily Simon. The gymnasium, Sports Hall, astroturf, floodlights and exercise suite have all opened up new opportunities.

The School's House system and inter-House matches are a wonderful way of giving pupils the joy and stress of competition. Girls of all ages are mixed together, which is good for the school community. Seniors are given an early introduction to captaincy, which involves offering strong support and refereeing, a

---

Left: Ling Association Swedish Gymnastics badge awarded to Alumna Margaret Coutts around 1916.

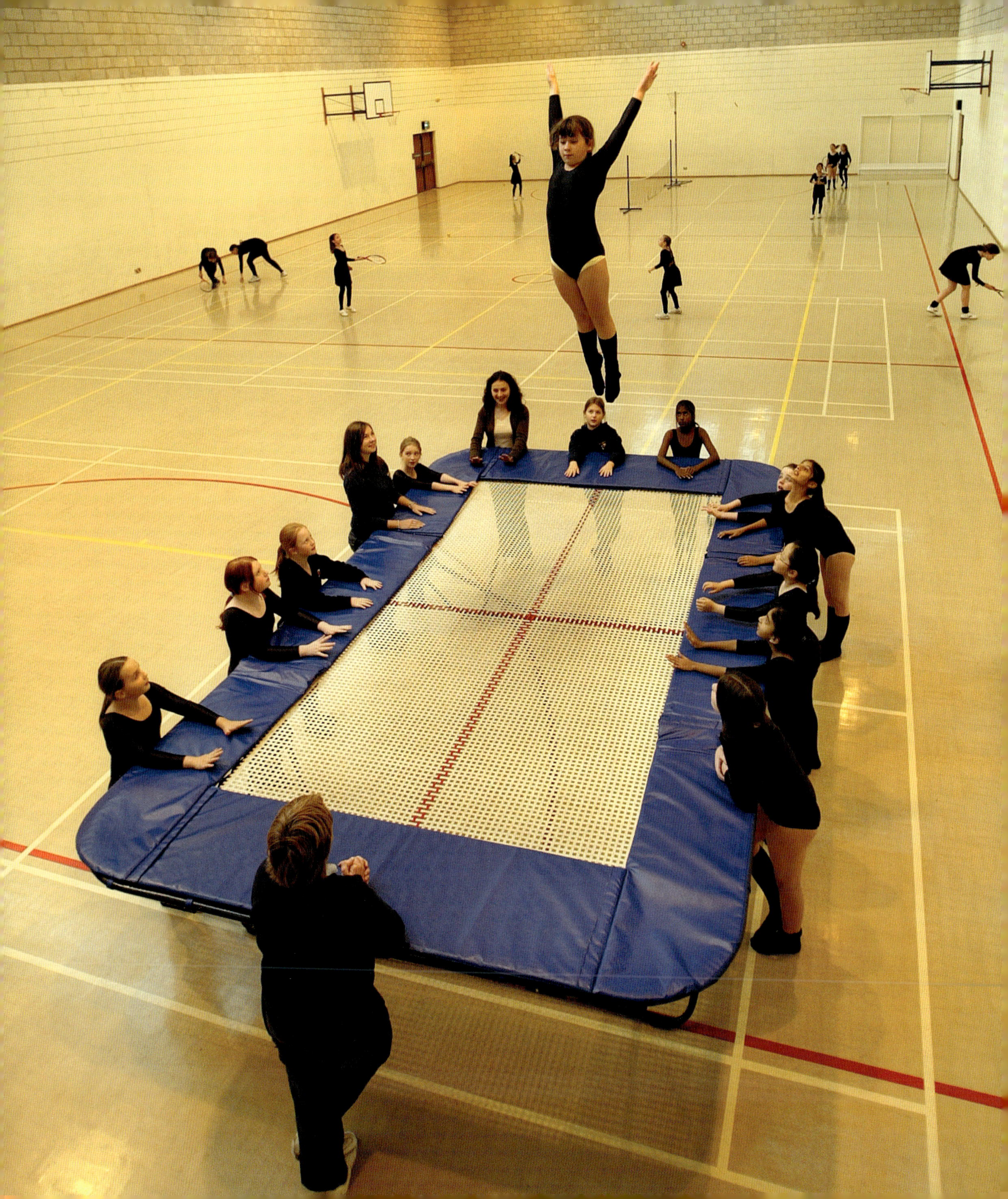

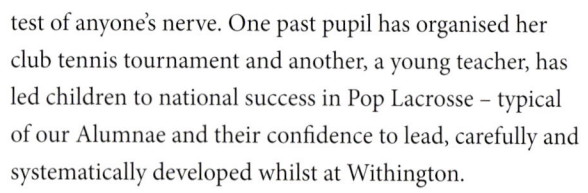

Clockwise from above: ready for hockey in the early 1920s and tennis in 1952, and après ski in 2004.

test of anyone's nerve. One past pupil has organised her club tennis tournament and another, a young teacher, has led children to national success in Pop Lacrosse – typical of our Alumnae and their confidence to lead, carefully and systematically developed whilst at Withington.

In 1908 school matches were played in cricket, tennis, lacrosse and hockey. We can pride ourselves that this important experience for our keenest games players continues. There have been some exceptional team successes over the years: our tennis team won the Midland Bank Under 15 National Championship three times in the 1980s, while the Senior tennis players reached the final group in the Aberdare Cup in 12 consecutive years. The results reflect individual and family effort as well as loyalty and commitment to Withington. Our lacrosse teams have won at regional level in all age groups and have been to the national finals on several occasions. Numerous individual honours across many sports are well documented each year in the School's *Newsletters*.

I began teaching at WGS in 1981 after my own private school education, training at Bedford College of Physical Education, and teaching at Sherborne School for Girls and a secondary modern in Plymouth (not forgetting seven years at home with children). My initial shock at finding myself in such a highly motivated and receptive environment soon faded as I tried to rise to the many challenges, recognising the golden opportunity of teaching some girls from seven years of age through to 18. In fact, I had 14 such groups, and many members of staff share that fulfilling experience.

In 1982 Sheila Bradford's arrival as Head of Geography heralded the introduction of the ski trip. Ably supported by her husband Michael, a Professor at Manchester University, Sheila led 21 holidays with many of us happily accompanying them. I admired the respect Sheila gave everyone we met on our trips and hope our pupils learned the value of building these good

Sports Day

As we celebrate our 125th anniversary it is fantastic to be able to say that, in line with the Founders' vision for the School, there is still more physical exercise and practical work than usual here at Withington. By far the biggest event of the sporting year is Sports Day. With the names of the Founders still at its heart in the names of the Houses – Herford, Lejeune, Scott and Simon – Sports Day is the final event in the House calendar, and often the most crucial for the House trophies. It's an opportunity, as it has always been, for the most able pupils to show off their sporting talents, and a chance for the less sportingly gifted to give their all for their House in true Withingtonian style!

The first Sports Day, or "Athletics Afternoon", as it was then called, was organised by Miss Parsons on Thursday 4th July 1968, when the four Houses competed for a trophy donated by Terry Taylor. It had actually been scheduled for the day before but was postponed, much like recent Sports Days, by the Manchester rain! For the first few years the Juniors and Seniors competed together in 30 different events, unlike today where separate Sports Days see the Seniors competing in 15 more traditional athletics events, and the Juniors in 13 less traditional ones, including egg and spoon, potato and obstacle races.

In 1969 the Mile Cup was introduced, and for the first three years was held by Ruth Adams. The first record of the winning time was 6:05s in 1973 by Karen Idowu. This ever popular event remains at the heart of Sports Day today, and the 2013 holder, Flora Whyte, recorded a time of 5:04s, over a minute quicker than the first. In more recent years girls have spent the summer term working hard to break and set new Withington athletics records, most notably in 2010, when Julia McCarthy set a new Third Form 200m time of 28.62 seconds, breaking a 29-year record held by Charlotte Goldberg. On a slightly less sporting and record-breaking note, after the 1976 Sports Day the staff had their own mini Olympics, and to top this the Upper Sixth provided a celebratory meal.

One of the more significant modern-day changes has been the venue. When astroturf was being installed on the school playing fields in 2000 Sports Day needed a temporary venue. Longford Park Athletics Stadium was chosen, and due to its fitting atmosphere and fantastic opportunity for our most talented athletes to perform to their best ability on a rubberised "tartan" track, Sports Day has remained there ever since. Despite these changes a lot remains the same, in particular the true Withington spirit which has shone through since the beginning and which we hope will continue to shine for years to come.

Jessica Richards

Gymnastics in the 1950s and 2010s.

though brief relationships. Skiing is immense fun, even for poor performers, and some of our less "gamesy" girls picked up this alternative form of exercise very well. How amazing that we managed to include visits to Venice and San Francisco!

Also dating from 1982 is the gymnastic display, although I notice there was one in 1920. This idea was inspired by my college days as well as the need to channel the Junior girls' energy through the long winters (before the days of the Sports Hall and the astroturf pitch). Over the years the display has become more polished, and several girls have performed sequences breathtaking in their flexibility, imagination and teamwork. The PE department hope that all young pupils enjoy the fun of performing for an audience, with the bonus that the exceptional girls have the chance to showcase their movements.

Swimming lessons in the summer term were established before my arrival, and I applaud the time and effort involved in organising and delivering this important life skill. It is vital that all our pupils have the chance to swim, and everyone in the Junior School and Third Form takes part in a gala at the end of term. Again, more talented girls have the challenge of the formal races, while girls with less experience dive for pennies or take part in novelty races. Everyone earns points for their House, which adds to the total involvement and pleasure.

In 1984 Fiona Clucas joined the PE department and was quick to ask Miss Hulme if she could take the Lower Fourth on

CHAPTER SEVEN • SPORTING LIFE

Sasha Carter and the Olympic Torch

Sasha Carter left Withington in 2011, and is currently studying medicine at the University of Leeds. Medicine is not her only interest, however; she has competed at national level in trampolining, and achieved second and third places in two Junior World Championships. In 2012 she carried the Olympic torch in Bolton – on her 19th birthday! Despite this huge honour and her success in her sport, Sasha remains grounded, remembering all that Withington gave her and its support for girls in their extra-curricular interests. Sasha hopes to work in medicine for a long time to come, and also to continue her trampolining success. She is currently aiming to compete in the Rio de Janeiro Olympic Games in 2016, and everyone here will be behind her all the way, hoping to see her shine and bring a medal home for Great Britain!

Brittany Fanning

It was an early start from home to head for a stretch of Chorley Old Road in Bolton to see Sasha carry the Olympic torch. The torch left the town centre at 6am and I was in place in good time to see Sasha on her four hundred metres of destiny, timed for around 6.40am. A huge number of friends and family, including friends from school, had turned out to support her – I seemed to be the only person without a "Sasha" T-shirt – and the anticipation was palpable. We could see and hear the cavalcade approaching, the sponsor's wagon belting out rousing tunes and dishing out freebies, shortly followed by the golden bus from which Sasha jumped at her allotted spot.

Sasha was surrounded and it was an emotional time for her family and her two younger sisters in particular. There were a few minutes for photos before "the kiss", the moment when Sasha took the Olympic flame and carried it off on part of its journey around the country. Sasha was beaming, beautiful, almost laughing aloud. A dream come true for a potential future Olympic trampolinist, on her 19th birthday, selected to be a torchbearer for the London 2012 games! All too soon she jogged off into the distance with the cheers of the crowd recognising that we had just witnessed history. A true Withingtonian, recognised for her talent, service to her community and her Olympic dream.

Mhairi Ferrol

109

an activity trip to the Isle of Man. So began excursions which led on to include France and even the warm waters of Greece, with activities including canoeing and windsailing. Many girls try such outdoor activities on Junior School trips, but the variation from the basic school timetable added to being on holiday together makes these excursions particularly valuable.

Fiona Clucas and I worked together for 17 years. One advantage of this stable situation was that we could organise regional events for schools in the north-west, including a tennis event for Under 11 girls and, in the 1990s, the Independent Schools Athletics Championships for Under 11, 12, 13 and 14 girls. Our pupils were always ready to assist and learn from the experience.

In 1986 came our first games tour, when a lacrosse group of 20 girls travelled to the USA. This had involved two years of planning and fundraising, and upgrading our sportswear. It is difficult now to appreciate what a big step this trip was. No one had mobile telephones or e-mail facilities so it was a much more adventurous time for young people, I think. They had to sort problems out together rather than send the quick text home that is now the fall-back solution. Teachers had to plan match arrangements ahead from one state to another, and meeting up each morning had to be thought through before we parted to stay with families around the town. I remember Washington DC as a special challenge due to the extensive nature of the Smithsonian Museum, but we all managed.

We have many amazing memories of our time in New York, Philadelphia, Baltimore and Long Island. Our American friends were used to practising on a daily basis, whereas we squeezed in a weekly session and fortnightly matches: different approaches to meet the needs of our particular education and university demands. Back in the 1980s we English were impressed by the number of bathrooms in an American house, not to mention the size of fridges and cornflakes packets!

Two further lacrosse tours followed and later hockey and netball players enjoyed trips to Malta, Canada, Australia and South Africa. We relished the camaraderie on the tours, the experience of foreign countries and the positive effect on our performance levels.

On a smaller scale, but no less enjoyable, have been our trips to the Wimbledon Championships. I played in the Junior

CHAPTER SEVEN • SPORTING LIFE

Above: alumnae Michelle Goulty and Claire Nance captain, respectively, the Oxford and Cambridge lacrosse teams in 2007. Left: games colours badge awarded to Alumna Margaret Grant (Carrington) in 1950.

Championships circa 1966 so always approach Southfields with trepidation, though our school visits are generally remembered with satisfaction! Often it is the pupils' first experience of Wimbledon, which is very exciting for them, though Wimbledon can turn us all into "groupies"! Mrs Pickering's main moment was seeing Ilie Nastase just as mine was having my photograph taken with Fred Stolle and John Newcombe.

Since the 1990s more staff from outside the PE department have given time to school sport. Sometimes the interest is passing but still worthwhile, and pupils have benefited from academic teachers offering football, cricket and volleyball.

When I think back to my time at Withington many things make me smile. Two members of my first touring team to the USA, Suzannah Thornton and Sarah Christiansen, were to meet as opposing lacrosse captains when Oxford played Cambridge three years later, with 2005 team members Michelle Goulty and Claire Nance going on to replicate that honour, Claire captaining Cambridge and Michelle Oxford. I like to think that they epitomise academic rigour, physical excellence and the leadership qualities we strive to encourage.

The physical education colleges of the past have changed dramatically; for one thing, single sex institutions are less popular than they were. Whatever the politicians throw at us in terms of new demands or making practical subjects sound more academic for reasons best known to themselves, we can be certain of one thing: WGS will continue to provide the balance to intellectual learning that physical education affords.

When I left Withington in 2005 I knew school sport was in the capable hands of Mhairi Ferrol and Sally Fletcher.

Denise Parnell

Denise Parnell is one of only 12 International female gold badge tennis referees in the world. As well as her essential role in organising international tennis events she is responsible for overseeing other aspects of each event such as sponsorship, communications and player liaison. She is also assistant referee at Wimbledon and a tennis consultant to IBM. Denise's sporting career started very early. She was guided by her parents, themselves world silver ice skating medallists, and involved in sport throughout school. Her Headmistress, Miss Hulme, supported her developing tennis career, allowing time off for training and competitions. Denise decided to become a tennis professional in 1978, after being taken to the Wimbledon Ladies' Final and setting her sights on playing at the event. At 18 she left Withington, bypassing university to start playing professionally at home and abroad.

As well as giving support, Withington instilled in Denise a life-long sense of self-belief and determination. This continued influence shows in the "four Ps" by which she lives her life – professionalism, pace, pride and passion – and which have motivated her and inspired her throughout her career.

Lauren Woodhead

Mhairi Ferrol, current Head of Physical Education at Withington, takes up the story:

Mary Rawsthorn retired from teaching at Withington in 2005, and much of her legacy continues to this day. Lacrosse is a "minority" sport in terms of numbers playing and its spread across the country but we, and particularly Miss Jessica Richards, are proud to maintain the tradition of offering it as a curricular and extra-curricular sport, and the girls very much enjoy its unique challenge. Tennis has recently been under the capable stewardship of Mrs Kate Orme and our teams consistently reach regional levels in the nationwide AEGON tournaments.

The organisation of our practice sessions is one of the major differences I have witnessed since joining Withington in 2002. Back then, all sessions took place at lunchtimes so that all girls could travel home on the school buses. The advent of floodlighting for the astroturf and netball courts, however, brought a shift of focus, and there are now weekly hour-long sessions for every Senior School pupil in hockey, netball and lacrosse, in addition to the ever-increasing programme of matches.

CHAPTER SEVEN • SPORTING LIFE

In September 2012 our largest-ever GCSE physical education group began study, with nine students. GCSE PE has at times been considered by parents and some staff "not academic enough" for Withington, but the theoretical and practical assessments make it challenging, exciting and rewarding for the pupils.

In 2009 the gymnasium was updated to feel more like a dance studio, and the aubergine décor and mirrored walls are certainly more contemporary than the traditional gymnasium style which we, our parents and, in some cases, our grandparents remember from the past. Mrs Pickering was determined that we should have a fitness suite, and girls from the Upper Fourth upwards enjoy lessons using state-of-the-art equipment. Academic, catering, maintenance, cleaning and office staff all make use of the suite, and recently Head of Music Gilly Sargent and I have been working out together to prove that music and PE are compatible!

Chloe Vell

Chloe, a student at Withington at the time of writing, has been involved in sport throughout her time at the School and studied PE at GCSE level. Although she enjoys many sports, including netball and athletics, her main focus is horse riding. She started riding at the age of three when her parents took her for lessons at a local riding school and got her first pony at seven. Chloe's potential became evident when she began to take part in local shows, and she started her international dressage career for Great Britain at the age of 12. Two years later she was National Champion: the youngest person ever to win at Stoneleigh Park. Chloe was selected for the Junior Great Britain team in the European Championships 2013, held in France. Following all this success, Chloe was approached by the equestrian magazine *Horse and Hound*, and now writes a fortnightly blog for their website.

Olivia Harman

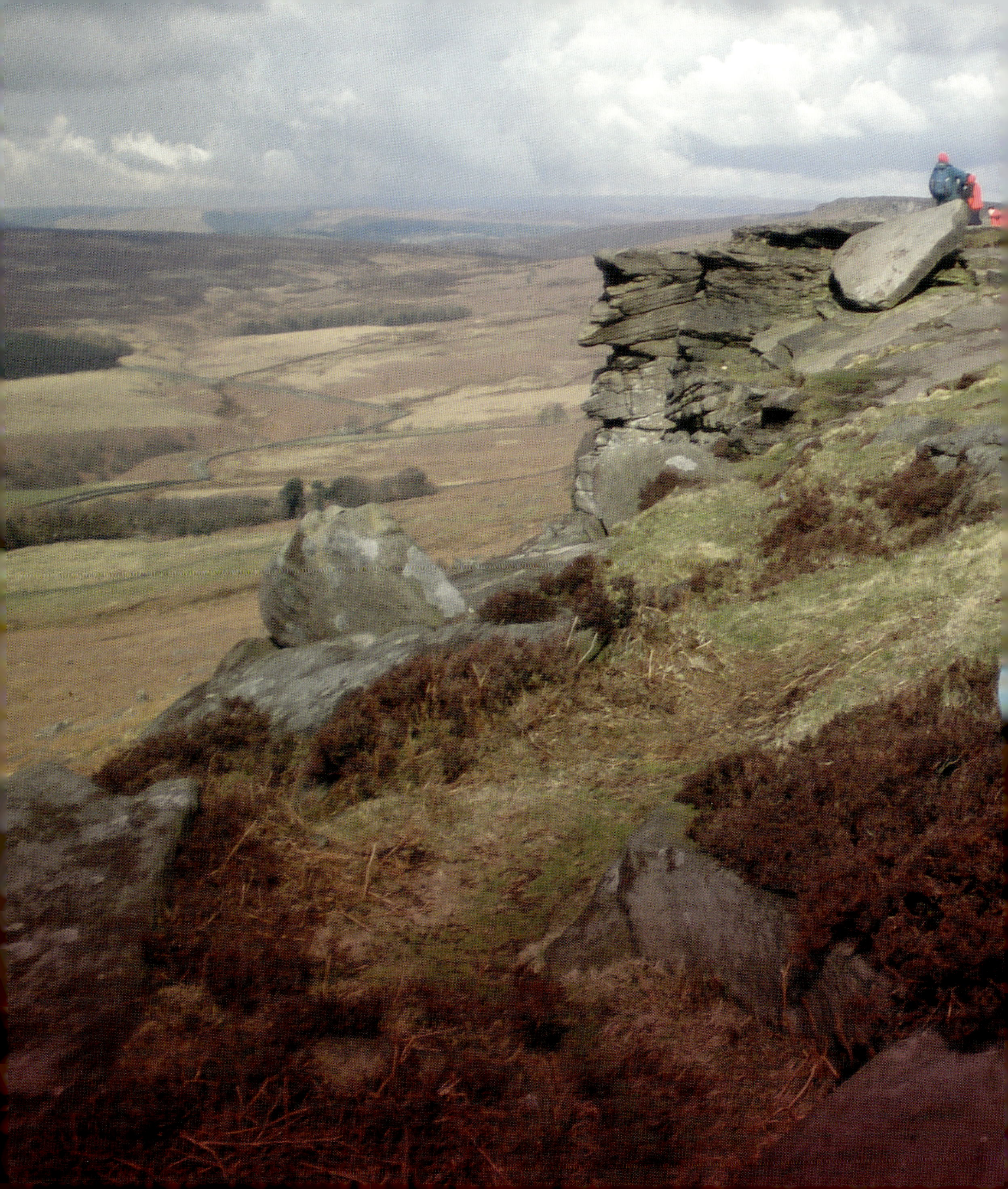

3 The Work of Life

"The general aim of the School will be to develop the faculties of the pupils, both intellectual and physical, so as to enable them to continue their own education after they have left school, and to prepare them for the work of life."

– THE FIRST MINUTE BOOK OF MEETINGS OF THE FOUNDERS, 1889

Chapter Eight

OUTSIDE THE CLASSROOM

Nadine West

"The general atmosphere and spirit of the School is delightful."

– 1924 INSPECTORS

From the School's earliest days, the commitment to forming a community focused not solely on academic endeavour but also on the girls' wider experience was clear. The Founders wanted the School to "develop the faculties of the pupils … to prepare them for the work of life". This ethos contributed, from its foundation documents onward, to the flourishing of a community which has never forgotten that the "work of life" is a broad one, enhanced by embracing opportunities to learn in many more ways than those dictated by examination syllabuses.

Withington girls enjoy being occupied. From the first moments of a visit to the School, the atmosphere of lively activity is clear; girls take full advantage of their time before school, at lunch breaks and after school to embrace extra-curricular activities, as well as learning in its more conventional form. Indeed, for both girls and staff, the lines between extra-curricular and curriculum activity are often unclear, as the palpable enthusiasm of the staff for pastimes which complement their academic knowledge often leads them to form societies which draw on and enhance classroom work. One may learn about recipes found in Roman documents, or understand classical clothing fashions from illustrations in textbooks, but drop into a Classics Club meeting and the infectious enthusiasm of ten Third Form girls styling themselves in laurels and togas and assuming poses inspired by classical artwork, all the while snacking on a Roman cake

Only at Classics Club … a lion lends a helping paw with a toga.

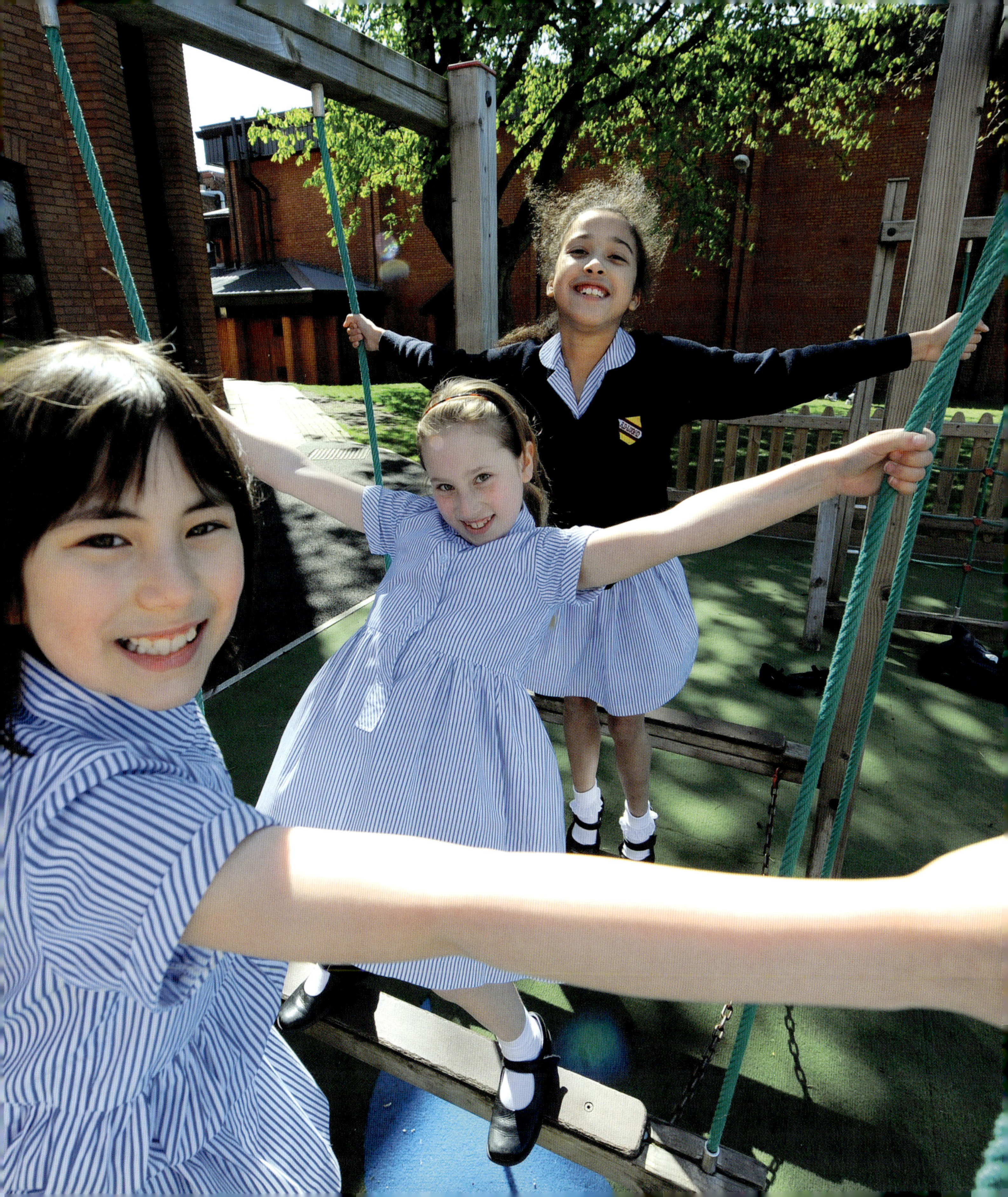

Ghyll Head

Withington enjoys a tradition of Third Form residential trips to the Lake District. Old *Newsletters* recall the fun of weekends camping at Lakeside, and, while we no longer camp, the purpose remains the same: getting to know each other and fostering team skills in an atmosphere of respect for self and others. The fond memories of Upper Sixth Formers and their excitement at returning as Peer Supporters testify to the trips' success, and friendships formed so early on are a valuable part of our induction programme.

Ghyll Head is an ideal setting. The spectacular lakeland scenery provides many opportunities for learning about the local wildlife and environment, whether exploring with torches on night walks or lying on our backs looking up at the stars. The grounds provide endless scope for games and adventures, and while some may regret the retirement of the infamous tree and vividly remember scaling up to the platform, the new climbing tower makes the zip wire accessible to all, and the experience has lost none of its adrenalin-charged thrills. Equally enjoyable is time spent on the lake, and the teamwork involved in constructing rafts for expeditions to deserted shores and uninhabited islands. Close collaboration and encouragement are vital as we seek to scramble up a local ghyll without getting wet, although often the option of jumping into a plunge pool or standing under a waterfall proves irresistible. One of the highlights of our stay is the nightline, where girls use teamwork to move along a path under cover of darkness, and many are the tales of strange apparitions and noises in the dark. There is tangible relief as we return triumphantly to the welcoming sight of the house and the prospect of hot chocolate.

Yorke Menzies

made in the food technology rooms, will remind any observer that sometimes the best fun – and the best learning – happens during the lunch break.

The earliest documents in the school archive show this love of extra-curricular activity taking shape from the end of the 19th century. Girls and staff relished the opportunity to be further informed about their world. Withington has always taken full advantage of the world-class universities on its doorstep, and of the thriving intellectual life of Manchester as a world-class city; indeed, one of the earliest lunchtime pursuits featured regular lectures by professors from what was then the Victoria University of Manchester. Topics were eclectic: examples include Greek Women in the Art of Antiquity, Babylon in the Time of Abraham, A Martial History of The East, and, perhaps most intriguingly, Some Queer Fishes, illustrated by a series of lantern slides depicting the fishes in all their splendour.

The most enduring evidence of this playful and somewhat eccentric approach to wider learning for the sheer joy of it comes in the form of the School Society. Founded in 1890, the School Society survived for more than a century in

Debating does matter: the victorious WGS team at 2012/13's contest.

almost unchanged form. Pupils attended the Society to listen to lectures but also to participate in informal and formal debate about the issues of the age, to perform readings and excerpts from works of literature, and to present essays about their interests, which initially encompassed the worlds of the sciences, arts and humanities.

By the 1960s the remit had refined itself and the focus of "The School Literary and Debating Society" had shifted to culture and the arts. The underpinnings of Withington's strong tradition of debating and public speaking can be clearly seen here. Matters of the day were – and still are – the focus of the girls' debates. Motions such as "This generation doth protest too much" and "The Trade Union movement has no place in modern Britain" characterised the 1970s, and "Computers will inherit the earth" and "The issue of AIDS" the 1980s. The motion "This house approves of Donny Osmond and all he stands for" from 1972 demonstrates that fun and popular culture are all part of the debating experience.

Girls debated for the intrinsic rewards of the format, but also competed publicly, first in the annual entry into the Didsbury Rotarians Public Speaking competition and later in the Mace championships. The School's focus on public speaking continued to diversify: the establishment of the Sir Rhys Davies Mock Trial event in the 1990s gave speakers a real-life format in which to hone their rhetorical skills, and continues to do so. In recent years, girls have expanded into debating competitions which focus on specific areas of knowledge, such as the Geographical Society Debates and the Modern Foreign Languages competition, which requires meaningful argument in French, German or Spanish. The Debating Society itself continues to flourish, with popular weekly meetings leading to entry into the Cambridge Union, Mace and Debating Matters competitions. Indeed, in 2013 the School achieved notable national and international success, with its teams being crowned first national and then international champions at the finals of the Debating Matters competition in London.

Current national and international champion and Withington student Sheanna Patelmaster says:

Model United Nations in session

> *Throughout my time in Debating Society I've watched fellow students who were nervous in the run-up to a debate overcome these feelings to give a fantastic performance and it is always a privilege to see. The highlight of my time in debating is undoubtedly the International Final of the Debating Matters Competition at the Battle of Ideas because it brought home exactly why debating is so important. Watching adult professionals debating such current issues reminded me that debating allows an argument to be examined from all angles and usually helps you to find some common middle ground and work out the most sensible compromise after the debate itself is over.*

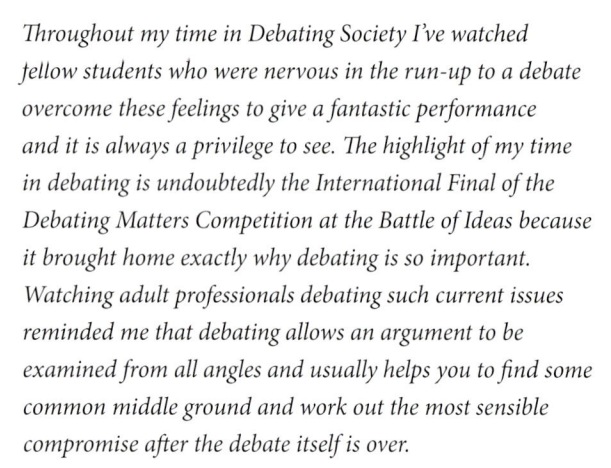

In the 1990s a new form of verbal battle began to creep into the School's familiar lexicon: Model United Nations (MUN). Initially a small and experimental day's discussion taking place at Manchester Town Hall and attended by a handful of girls, the activity grew rapidly in popularity and Withington teams made their debut at MUN at Cheadle Hulme in 2001. This fixture was to become an annual one, and when in 2006 Cheadle Hulme's director of MUN, Ms Jane Maher, was appointed as the Head of History at WGS, the stage was set for rapid and enthusiastic expansion. Girls now compete nationwide and internationally, achieving success in The Hague, Bath, London and indeed at our own conference, which has become a popular destination for delegates from around the country.

MUN is a rigorous and demanding experience. Participants must typically research three or four world issues from the perspective of an assigned Member State of the UN, and then work within a large and combative committee to push through their solutions to international problems. Public speaking skills are not sufficient; the MUN forum tests the skills of initiative, rapid response to the unexpected, and networking ability to their utmost. Former Withington MUN delegate and chair Sophie Lloyd, now a solicitor, says:

> *My legal career is in its infancy, but it is already clear to me how experiences throughout my 11 years at Withington, such as Model United Nations, helped prepare me for the challenges I face in my working life. I use the skills I developed at MUN on a daily basis today when advising clients and negotiating their position against the other side,*

or presenting and explaining interesting legal issues I have come across to senior colleagues. Going through the process of overcoming the apprehension that surrounds public speaking and debating is invaluable at a stage in life where interviews for university and jobs are fast approaching. I realise how lucky I was to go to a school that provided me with the opportunity to develop the confidence to stand my ground in any debate, no matter which side I might be asked to represent.

As well as in the sphere of public speaking, the legacy of the School Society lives on in other ways within the current extra-curricular life of the School. Writing across the range of forms, including essays, journalism and creative genres, was initially chiefly a feature of this society, with a silver cup being purchased and awarded internally for the finest writing in any given year. The love of writing has now become much more part of the whole-school ethos. Creative writing clubs are flourishing as an extra-curricular aspect of the English department, with students' work winning prizes in a range of competitions including a recent unprecedented first and third place in the Readers' Digest Short Fiction competition in 2010. In 2011, recent Alumna Miriam Battye achieved the extraordinary feat of being placed third in the Bruntwood Prize for new dramatic writing at the tender age of 19, with a piece which had its genesis in work begun while still at school.

The school newspaper, *Scrawl*, came off the presses for the first time in 2007 and has since become a termly highlight, drawing contributions from girls across the age range and edited by a talented group of Sixth Form students under the guidance of Ms Christine Davies, the Head of English. Lively and often provocative, the newspaper allows girls to write news, opinion pieces, poetry and more lighthearted submissions for their peers. This celebration of the written word thrives elsewhere too: young writers have opportunities to meet published authors, including Alumna Emma Chapman, who visited the School in 2013 to discuss her critically acclaimed first novel *How to be a Good Wife*. The year 2014 saw the School

Emma Chapman

Emma Chapman loves books and reading. She believes "books offer an insight into other people that you rarely get from talking to them." After leaving Withington in 2004, Emma studied English literature at Edinburgh University before completing an MA in creative writing at Royal Holloway. She recalls her first attempt at writing fiction: a novel, inspired by a Keats poem, about a maths professor and an artistic dreamer who fall in love, full of clichés. But she went on to be at the centre of a literary bidding war for the rights to her debut novel *How to be a Good Wife*, published in 2013. Some of Emma's fondest memories are from Withington, meeting the people who are still her closest friends and developing a love for the arts. Originally it was drama which inspired Emma, and while at school she wanted to be an actress for the same reasons she now loves writing. Emma hopes to continue travelling and improving her writing skills, and before pursuing her next project plans to read "everything I've ever wanted". Emma's Founders' Day choice was a collection of Don McCullin's war photography.

Theodora Critchley

Playing with words: Latin Scrabble.

planning its first residential visit to the prestigious Arvon Foundation, taking a group of talented young writers to spend a week working on their short story writing skills under the tuition of published authors, a venture generously supported by the Withington Annual Fund.

Debate, essay writing and the negotiation of contentious issues does not stop, however, at the door of the arts and humanities. Harking back to the first days of the School, Withingtonians pursue a range of extra-curricular lectures, discussion groups and seminars across the academic spectrum with, tellingly, attendance never limited to students – or indeed staff – who pursue those subjects within the classroom. One of the most well-attended extra-curricular groups in the weekly calendar is PhilSoc, the series of lectures based on contemporary scientific issues and hosted jointly between Withington, Manchester High School for Girls and Manchester Grammar School.

Originally an occasional joint venture, inaugurated in 1993 and attended by a handful of girls, PhilSoc now meets every Friday during term time and continues the tradition of tapping into the local universities' huge treasure trove of knowledge. Noted scientists from Manchester, Liverpool, Leeds and beyond come to present their findings to a vocal and enthusiastic audience of students from the three schools. The visit from popular television presenter and academic Professor Brian Cox is remembered particularly fondly; in 2008 WGS girls were fortunate enough to hear him lecture on the issues of nuclear energy and the work conducted at CERN, and the staff attending describe the experience as inspirational for themselves and the girls alike.

Of course, the wonders of the universe, and indeed the natural world, cannot fully be appreciated from behind a microscope nor in front of a PowerPoint presentation. Whether

A staff of many talents – Strictly *comes to Withington.*

it be scientific curiosity or just a desire to see cows in their natural habitat and then run away from them, Withington girls have another avenue to allow them to commune with biology: the Duke of Edinburgh's Award Scheme. For much of the late 20th century the School enjoyed the beauty of the local countryside through its Hiking Club, a group of keen outdoorswomen who ventured to the Peak District, Pennines, North Wales and the Lake District for weekend and holiday hiking. However, in the 1980s, a few students asked for the School's support with starting up a Duke of Edinburgh's Award Scheme, and today it is without doubt the most popular extra-curricular activity in WGS's extensive programme, with almost every girl in the Sixth Form having experienced the Scheme during her time at Withington.

Initiative, planning, group management: these abilities are all honed by the experience the Award offers but, at Withington, they certainly aren't confined by it. On Wednesday afternoons after a long day's lessons, debaters may be found arguing over the fine points of rhetoric at one end of the School and Duke of Edinburgh participants planning route cards at the other, but somewhere between the two lies the base of the entrepreneurs: at WGS, future Anita Roddicks and Hilary Deveys can launch their very first attacks on the free market by participating in the Young Enterprise scheme. Overseen by Madame Catherine Ositelu, the YE scheme is a national competition for students in the Lower Sixth Form to devise a product, raise funds for its manufacture, craft marketing and sales strategies and then manage the sales of the product. Profit is the goal, but presentation skills are also vital, as the teams must compete with others in front of a "Dragon's Den" final as well as competing in a trade fair, where sales tactics are essential.

The long-term project of devising a product that is genuinely innovative, conducting market research, balancing budgets and working together as a team is clearly a challenging one, and it is testament to the girls' abilities and the high quality of support they receive that a Withington team has taken at least one award at every regional trade fair in the last five years. Teams also enjoy the School's tradition of inventive naming: Ululati, KRE8OR, Diversa and Ugly have all taken on the market forces of Manchester in the last ten years, and the experience of promoting a product allows girls with business and managerial skills to hone their talents in a hugely creative and enjoyable forum.

The Duke of Edinburgh's Award Scheme

The Duke of Edinburgh's Award Scheme (DofE), established personally by the Duke in 1956, has outdoor expeditions at its heart but encompasses much more. It requires young people not only to plan and execute an expedition, but also to show commitment to the wider community through volunteer work and demonstrate self-improvement through a skill such as a sport, musical instrument, artistic discipline or other personal challenge.

The story of the Scheme at Withington provides a good example of pupil initiative. Girls had been involved in the Scheme outside school for a while when in 1984 a Lower Sixth pupil, Michele Kilgore, asked for the School's support with taking on an Award group. Mrs Sheila Bradford, Head of Geography, became unofficial staff facilitator and the inaugural group had 17 members. From these small beginnings participation swiftly increased and by the late 1980s, the School had become formally involved. Ms Lucille Holden took up the organisational baton, followed by Mrs Ruth Lindsay-Dunn.

The experience of the Bronze Award has become something of a rite of passage for most girls in the Lower Fifth as they discover how to wrangle with an Ordnance Survey map, craft a realistic route card and negotiate the art of cooking noodles on a Trangia stove. The north-west, never known for its mild and sunny climate, can be a fickle friend to DofE expeditions, and 25 years' worth of *Newsletter*s feature generations of girls bemoaning the weather. Nevertheless, the experience inspires real pride and satisfaction within the school community. This pride is well deserved: thousands of young people begin the Award every year in countries around the globe, but relatively few proceed to the Silver and Gold phases. Gold Award recipients have typically completed at least a year's volunteering, a similar period of time developing a physical skill and one

CHAPTER EIGHT • OUTSIDE THE CLASSROOM

other skill, a five-day expedition in what must be "wild country", and a five-day residential activity to increase their self-reliance and independence. They have until they are 25 to complete this programme. Withington girls often complete their Gold Award while still at school – a remarkable achievement.

Between 2000 and 2012 Mrs Lindsay-Dunn organised, encouraged, cajoled and supported over 850 girls towards an impressive 482 Bronze, 177 Silver and 77 Gold Awards, and the numbers continue to mount. She reflects fondly on her leadership of the scheme:

> Valuable lessons are learned: tolerance of others, map reading and navigation skills, team work, cooperation and leadership. It is rewarding to see girls getting out of their comfort zone, realising what they are capable of achieving, and gaining maturity and confidence. Most of them commit to at least one activity that requires them to turn up regularly and on time and work with other people, such as leading Brownie groups or doing charity work. Nearly all the girls genuinely enjoy the sessions and the expeditions and pass on their enthusiasm to younger girls, hence the ongoing popularity of the scheme.

When the School was awarded "DofE Beacon" status in 2008, Mrs Lindsay-Dunn and Mrs Pickering attended a Gold Award Ceremony at St James's Palace, where they had the dual delight of meeting the Duke of Edinburgh in person and applauding presentations to four Withingtonians.

Janet Pickering and Nadine West

Wrangling with the map on a Duke of Edinburgh's Award Scheme expedition.

Of course, no overview of the extra-curricular life of the School would be complete without mention of the ever-changing cast of characters who provide affection, life lessons and indeed cuddles for the girls: Pets Club. Often cited by new Third Formers as a reason for selecting the School in the first instance, Pets' Club allows girls to take on the responsibility of caring for animals including hamsters, guinea pigs and stick insects. They tend to them on a daily basis, oversee the birth and nurture of the next generations, and, of course, mourn the passing of their favourite animals.

From Mosaic Club to App Development Club, Bridge Club to Graphic Novel Club, Withington's staff is one of many talents, all extended generously to the girls in the free time of both. Such commitment to extra-curricular activities is clear evidence of one of the School's abiding philosophies: that education, at its best, is seen not merely through the quantifying measure of examination results but rather as providing something more profound – the delight and joy which come from new opportunities and new skills, inside and outside the classroom.

125

Chapter Nine

MANCHESTER AND THE LOCAL COMMUNITY

Janet Pickering

"Treat others as you would like them to treat you."

– THE GOLDEN RULE

The Founders' general aim for the School, which opens this part of the book, stressed the importance of preparing its pupils for "the work of life". In keeping with this vision, the current aims of the School include the encouragement of "respect for self and others, developing strong links with parents, Alumnae and the local community".

The world in which the "work of life" of current pupils occurs is of course radically different from that of the late 19th century, as is the density and diversity of the School's local community. However, the focus on the "three Rs" – respect for self, respect for others and responsibility for actions – and on awareness of, and sensitivity towards, the needs of others remains fundamental to Withington's ethos.

As in Bach's aria, sheep could "safely graze" alongside the School when it relocated to Wellington Road in 1903, but not so today. The evolution of the School's premises and facilities is recorded in the first part of this book. From 1908 until the end of the 20th century, the four longest-serving Headmistresses ensured that Withington's developments kept pace with growing numbers of pupils and staff and with the changing educational landscape. Miss Grant (1908–1938), Miss Bain (1938–1961), Miss Hulme (1961–1985) and Mrs Kenyon (1986–2000) all brought imagination and great vision to their plans for School.

	The Golden Rule
Baha'i	He should not wish for others that which he doth not wish for himself. *From the writing of Baha'u'llah*
Buddhism	I will act towards others exactly as I would act towards myself. *From the Siglo-Vada Sutta*
Christianity	Whatsoever ye would that men should do to you, do ye even so to them. *Gospel according to St Matthew*
Confucianism	Do not do to others what you would not like for yourself. *From the Analects of Confucius*
Epictetus	What you would avoid suffering yourself, seek not to impose on others. *The Greek Philosopher, Epictetus*
Hinduism	This is the sum of duty: Do naught to others Which, if done to thee, could cause thee pain. *From the Mahabharata*
Islam	None of you 'truly' believe, until he wishes for his brothers what he wishes for himself. *A saying of the Prophet Muhammad*
Jainism	He should treat all beings as he himself should be treated. The essence of right conduct is not to injure anyone. *From the Suta-Kritanga*
Judaism	What is harmful to yourself, do not to your fellow men. *From Hillel: The Talmud*
Sikhism	As thou deemest thyself, so deem others. *From Guru Granth Sahib*

Opposite: Sugar Rush, 2012: sweet success for another triumphant charity fashion show.

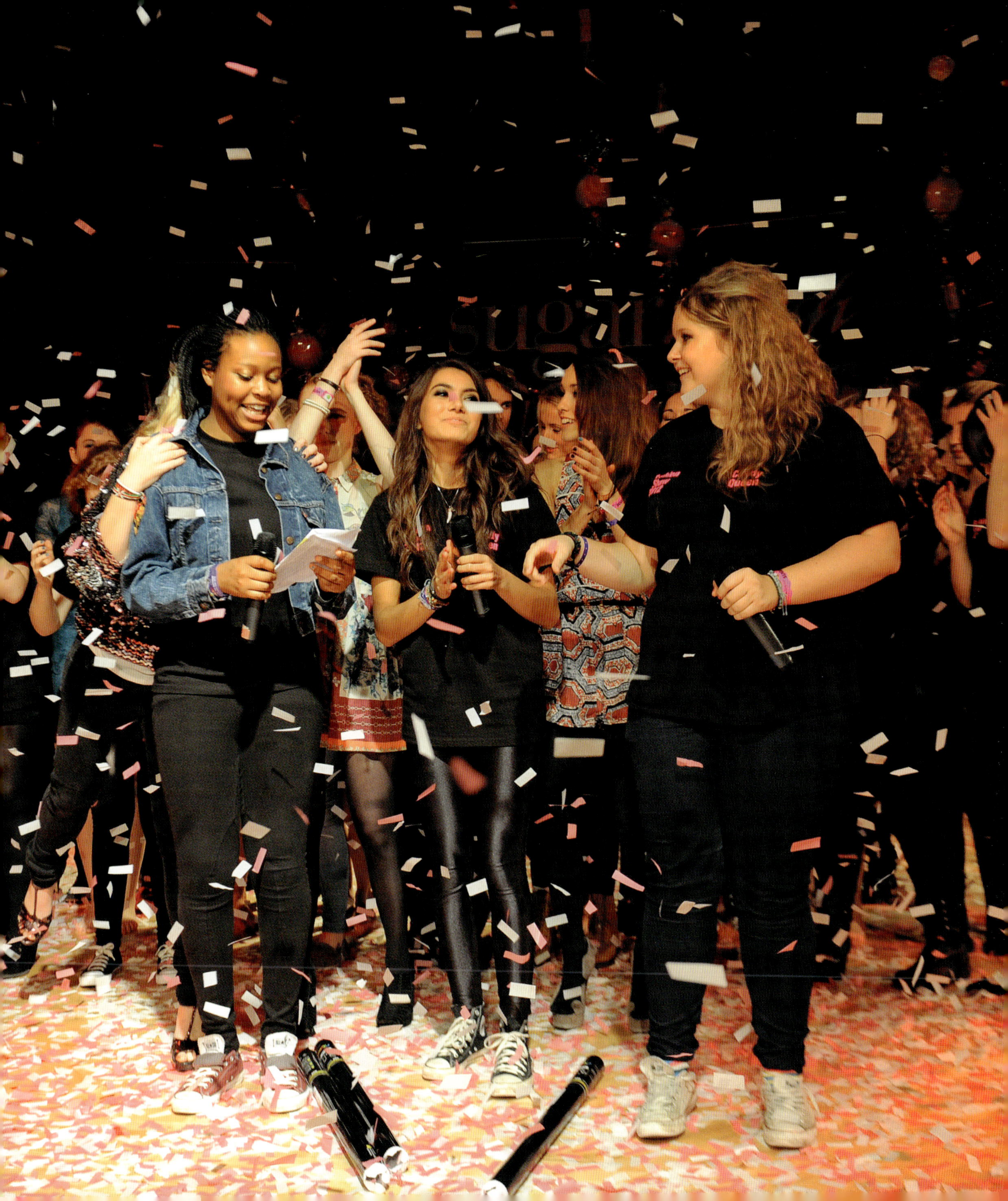

Stephen Whittle OBE

Stephen Whittle was a girl when he was a pupil at Withington, achieving the positions of Deputy Head Girl, House Captain and captain of cricket. At the age of 19 Stephen transitioned from female to male, and his determination and confidence have led to him being one of the most notable equality rights activists in Britain. In 2005, he received an OBE for his dedication to gender issues.

Stephen has not only been recognised in Britain however. In 2006, he was awarded the Virginia Prince Lifetime Achievement Award by the International Federation for Gender Education in the USA. Stephen is a law professor at MMU and his detailed knowledge of equalities law has allowed him to confront the government on key issues regarding gender and transsexual equality with conviction. Consequently, he has spearheaded a new political movement that contests body fascism.

From an early age, Stephen knew that he wanted to be a teacher and he has realised this dream. He had the strength of character to persevere when rejected by those who scorned and shunned him. He still endures abuse from some; however he has a natural academic flair and is a respected professor. Stephen's wife, Sarah, and his four children have supported him throughout his campaigning.

Stephen Whittle is a true role model. He stood up for what he believed in and had the bravery to speak out where others would have shrunk into the shadows. He is proud of who he is and now leads a happy and fulfilling life with his family.

Natalie Robinson

Mrs Kenyon often spoke about the School's innate modesty and its wearing of achievements lightly. Withington has never built for "flash and show" but always to provide facilities and resources to meet the needs of the pupils and the demands of an appropriately broad and challenging curriculum. And as it has evolved, the School has worked with and contributed to its local community in many ways.

The success of building projects over some 40 years was due in no small part to the empathy and continuity of the School's building design consultants: David Davies Associates and, later, Thomas Worthington Design. David Davies' passion for the School first became evident in the 1970s, when his daughter was in the Junior School; in times when every penny had to be counted, and accounted for, he marshalled a team of unpaid parent volunteers for decorating duty. Both practices addressed cohesion within the school building as it expanded and was in-filled. They retained original features where possible, meticulously checked the quality of materials, incorporated eco-friendly features, maintained an aesthetic balance to the external aspect, and even ensured that projects were completed on time and to budget, in spite of frequent add-on requests. Withington remains a "hidden jewel" in the locality; it makes its facilities available free of charge to various local groups, including the Fire Service and Salvation Army for reasons clear from my account of the 2003 fire in Chapter 3, the Civic Society, Rotarians and Incorporated Society of Musicians. The Sports Hall is hired most evenings by local student, community and business groups, and the Marjorie Hulme Arts Centre is used as a venue for local schools' concerts and prizegivings. For some time, free use of the Sports Hall in partnership with Manchester City Council enabled local teenage boys to receive weekly football coaching under the youth inclusion programme "Streetlife"; one season they won their league – under the name "Withington Girls' School"!

The School's links with the University of Manchester go back to the Founders. At the 21st "coming of age" celebrations in 1911, C.P. Scott described Adolphus Ward, former Principal of Owens College and Vice-Chancellor of the Victoria University,

CHAPTER NINE • MANCHESTER AND THE LOCAL COMMUNITY

The mosaic created by pupils for the Manchester Children's Hospital's Harrington Building, 2012.

Withingtonians were studying there with a further seven having already graduated. By 1931, Withingtonians were represented in every faculty, Peggy Williams was captain of the University Cricket Club, and four members of the lacrosse team came from the School. School records show that a total of 61 pupils entered the University up to 1945, 17 holding scholarships, and Manchester has appeared on the destination of leavers every subsequent year.

Many former and current WGS parents work or have worked at the University; PGCE students are offered initial teacher training at the School and many Sixth Form pupils have engaged in summer research projects, particularly during Dr Francisca Wheeler's tenure as Head of Physics. Several plaques in School bear the names of prominent members of the University. Most recently, in 2005, Professor Katharine Perera, then Chair of Governors of the School and Senior Pro-Vice-Chancellor of the University, opened the multimedia Language Laboratory and Professor Dame Nancy Rothwell, then Vice President of Research and now President and Vice-Chancellor of the University, opened the new science wing on a special Science Day that included a particle physics lecture by Professor Brian Cox. Professor Alan Gilbert, the first President and Vice-Chancellor of the merged University, opened the Sixth Form block in 2009 and, in resonance with Withington's founding principles, challenged the pupils to "use the precious inheritance of their education to help others through dangerous times".

University post-graduate students have helped with the "Four Schools" partnership programme involving science and mathematics staff and pupils from Withington, Manchester Grammar School and two local Academies. Through the government-backed Independent/State School Partnership programme (ISSP), Withington pupils have worked alongside those from Whalley Range High School on art and language projects and from Trinity School and the Northern Chamber Orchestra on music compositions. A year-long community partnership with the Manchester Children's Hospital culminated in October 2012 with the unveiling, by Sir Bobby Charlton, of a magnificent eight-foot mosaic, created by pupils,

as "the spiritual father" of Manchester University.[1] Adolphus Ward chaired the School Council during its first year, handing over to C.P. Scott; five of the subsequent Chairs, spanning a total of 50 years, have held senior positions at the University, and there has always been at least one representative from the University on the Governing Body. Both Miss Hulme and Mrs Kenyon served on the University Court and I am currently a member of the Assembly and Nominations Committee. University lecturers regularly give talks at the School, not least to the long-running PhilSoc, and pupils attend public lectures at the University. May Heyford is recorded as receiving a scholarship to Manchester University in 1909; by 1929, seven

Top: Classics Club, featuring Minimus the Mouse, at Old Moat Primary School. Bottom: Mrs Pickering pours copious quantities of tea at the Christmas party.

in the adjacent Harrington Building. The School benefits from Manchester's magnificent concert halls, theatres, galleries and sports facilities and pupils and staff, past and present, are always keen to volunteer for major events, such as the 2002 Commonwealth Games. Pupils engage in work experience with a number of local businesses, many of whom provide invaluable information at the biannual Careers Evenings, and business volunteers support Withington's Young Enterprise companies.

The range of extra-curricular activities covered in Chapter 8 varies, to some extent, according to specific enthusiasms of staff and pupils. One constant is the Duke of Edinburgh's Award Scheme: Nadine West and I have described its origins and enduring popularity at the School in previous pages. Bronze, Silver and Gold Awards require three or six, six or 12, and 12 or 18 months of regular voluntary work, respectively, with inevitable strengthening of links with local communities, in line with Withington's aims.

The girls' enthusiasm to help others is further testified by their eagerness to enrol on the Sixth Form Voluntary Service Scheme and devote some of their precious non-taught study time to assist in local hospitals, hospices, care homes for the elderly, nurseries, playgroups and schools, including those for pupils with profound learning, sensory, physical and communication difficulties. The longstanding link with Old Moat Primary School has involved Ms Holden and Sixth Formers teaching Latin to their Year 5 and 6 pupils, musicians, dancers and actors performing in their assemblies, joint full-day music and art projects and the hosting of their Sports Day.

One of the highlights of the school year remains the Christmas party, for over 30 years organised through the now-defunct Didsbury Rotary Club, which supported many Withington projects overseas and enabled generations of girls to engage in competitive public speaking. Since 2012, WGS has taken over responsibility for organising and hosting the event. On the day of the party, local senior citizens are transported to the Marjorie Hulme Arts Centre, where they are entertained by Withington musicians before enjoying copious quantities of tea, sandwiches and cake, prepared and served by pupils and staff in the dining room before returning, doggy bags in hand, to the Arts Centre for the distribution of presents (stories of fights over these are not entirely apocryphal) and community singing. The age range typically spans over 80 years, and the experience has a lasting impact on all those involved. In addition, many pupils organise their own voluntary placements and put in

"Latent knowledge and unusual powers" (Dr E.W. Barnes, 1930): fashion shows, miles of pennies, the WiGS Race for Life raise funds for charity.

many hours of hard work in local charity shops, youth centres, sports clubs and Scout and Brownie groups.

I know from the experience of accompanying Withington trips at home and overseas that the girls are A* shoppers and bargain hunters. However, they have also, throughout the School's history, shown themselves to be accomplished fundraisers. Every year, each Form group chooses a charity to support, and calories are consumed and raffle tickets bought while girls run, walk, swim, play, dance, sing, and engage in various high-adrenalin activities in return for sponsorship; stalls are set up, and a myriad of imaginative ways are used to raise annual totals averaging £20,000 since 2000. As detailed elsewhere, fundraising has helped school development and the Bursary Fund, but much has focused on local, national and international charities. The School has a particularly longstanding link with the local branch of Barnardo's, with many thousands of pounds raised over the years through the sell-out Fashion Shows, along with miles of pennies collected by the Junior School and countless other events. The mountains of produce collected each year for Junior and Senior School Harvest Festivals went to a food bank in Moss Side and a Parish in Salford in the 1980s, and more recently

Citizenship Day

Born in 2005 from the idea that the most effective way of delivering the then new Citizenship part of the Personal, Social and Health Education curriculum was through a whole-school event, Citizenship Day has become a much-loved and fulfilling annual fixture on Withington's busy calendar. At the heart of the day is the recognition that we are all part of a community, be it local or international, and that in serving others, as Mahatma Gandhi once said, we "find ourselves". Citizenship Day sees the School at its very best, with Lower Sixth girls mentoring and assisting the Third Form with their community projects; staff washing cars, running sports days or making lunches; and all pupils fully engaged and invigorated by helping and learning about others. We work with the Withington Civic Society, neighbouring primary schools, local retirement centres and The Christie Hospital; and thoroughly enjoy being a real part of our local community. Other year groups learn about the importance of Fair Trade or the work of the United Nations, and what it really means to be part of an international community. Citizenship Day is yet another event that helps thread together the wonderfully diverse Withington Girls' School tapestry.

Clara Edge

have supported the work of local charities such as the Booth Centre, which helps homeless people in Manchester. The Wood Street Mission supports children and families in Manchester and Salford affected by poverty; proceeds from staff pantomimes and musicals support their work and representatives from the charity participate in the annual Carol Service at St Ann's Church. St Ann's Hospice is another fundraising focus, and the annual WiGS fun run, the School's version of Race for Life, raises funds for The Christie charity to enable cancer research projects outside the scope of the NHS. Through school assemblies, speakers from these charities give the girls a wider appreciation of the hardship faced by others living close by, and make them ever more determined to help. The Christie also benefits from the now-annual Citizenship Days as does the Withington Civic Society, which works to improve the environment and amenities of the areas of Withington, Lady Barn and Old Moat.

Miss Hulme's foresight in 1974 in instigating the WGS Trust to support the School's capital development and the provision of means-tested bursaries is related in the first part of this book. When planning the School, the Founders had doubtless envisaged it would remain comfortably small, and would continue to serve what they described as "a superior neighbourhood". But, while it remains comfortably small in relative terms, much has changed in the School's immediate environment. WGS now sits at the heart of the Old Moat ward which, along with the Withington ward, is among the most deteriorated areas in Manchester both economically and in terms of access to health and education. In 2010, Manchester was classed as the second most deprived district in England out of a total of 326,[2] based on income deprivation. Since 2005, over 50 per cent of pupils receiving Bursary support have come from areas in Manchester which fall into the top one to five per cent most deprived areas in England. Initiatives such as the Saturday morning SHINE programme for gifted and talented pupils from state primary schools in socially and economically deprived areas and summer schools offering means-tested assisted places to local children form part of the School's outreach programme. Each year, given the level of over-subscription, Withington

Left: SHINE on a Saturday morning; above: fun socks for Children in Need.

could fill its places with full-fee payers, but social diversity is embedded in its ethos, as is the spread of nationalities, ethnic origins, race and religion. The composition of the pupil body reflects diversification within the School's catchment area, which essentially covers a 20-mile radius.

It is not easy to articulate Withington's unique atmosphere and ethos, but the warm, friendly, purposeful and happy environment in which each individual is well known and supported and willing to support others is readily identified by visitors, including inspection teams, whose most recent report notes a school that "operates as a harmonious and happy community with the minimum of rules".[3] After my first Open Day, when I had extolled the virtues of the School and the supportive, non-hierarchical relationships amongst pupils and between pupils and staff, the father of a prospective pupil asked his Fifth Form guide for the "real story" of what school life was like as a pupil; she turned to him and replied without hesitation, "At Withington everyone helps everyone else". The Withington community fosters mutual knowledge, understanding and tolerance. The Christian Education Movement (CEM) run by girls in the 1960s became "Revival", which in turn became the Christian Society in 1996. Separate Jewish, Muslim and Hindu Societies, organised and run by senior pupils with minimum staff oversight, were established in Mrs Kenyon's time, and their whole-school assemblies inform all pupils of their key festivals, beliefs and traditions. Immediately after the 9/11 attack on the World Trade Center, the Muslim Society Committee requested the opportunity to talk to the School about the dissociation of their faith from acts of terrorism. Pupils also learn about world faiths through the religious studies course and visits to local churches, mosques, synagogues and temples, initiated during Jane Deacon's 26 years as Head of the Department. *The Withington Hymn Book*, produced in 2004, contains readings and prayers from a broad range of faiths, including ten versions of the Golden Rule of treating others as you yourself would wish to be treated. WGS's ethos enshrines a positive appreciation of difference and its values equate to those of "good citizenship".

In 1930, at the opening of the School's new hall and classroom accommodation, Dr E.W. Barnes, Bishop of Birmingham and husband of Adolphus Ward's daughter, Adelaide, said "The development of girls' education during the last 50 years has released for the community latent knowledge and unusual powers of which we do not perceive".[4] He went on to affirm that the citizenship of women was a most important influence, and that we could not have too many highly educated women. Over 80 years on, Dr Barnes and the Founders would surely be content with Withington's links with Manchester and the local community, and with the social conscience of its highly educated pupils.

133

Chapter Ten

WITHINGTON AND THE WIDER WORLD

Julie Buckley

"He wished for all pupils a happy school life in and out of doors; holidays full of sunshine, over their heads and in their minds; and a return to school in fine spirits and with their hearts set on whatsoever was high and honourable and good."

– ADOLPHUS WARD'S ADDRESS TO THE SCHOOL'S ANNUAL SUMMER MEETING, 1893,
AS REPORTED BY THE *MANCHESTER GUARDIAN*

In 1890, Withington's Founders set out to create a school that would offer girls an education academically comparable to that available to boys at the time. Now, 125 years later, Withington remains remarkably faithful to its Founders' intention to provide an "interesting and stimulating" education.

A key element is the extension of education beyond the traditional classroom. In the last 25 years in particular, as the world has become increasingly globalised and interconnected, Withington has embraced the opportunity to explore and understand the changing environment the girls will live in as adults. Over these last 25 years WGS has encouraged the girls to venture out into the UK and beyond, observe new landscapes, experience cultural diversity, and get involved in exchanges and activities which make a positive impact on places or people. This has fostered eager curiosity and informed awareness amongst our school community, which doesn't stop

---

Right: at the Welland Canal, Canada, August 1939. Opposite: World Challenge, Namibia, 2007.

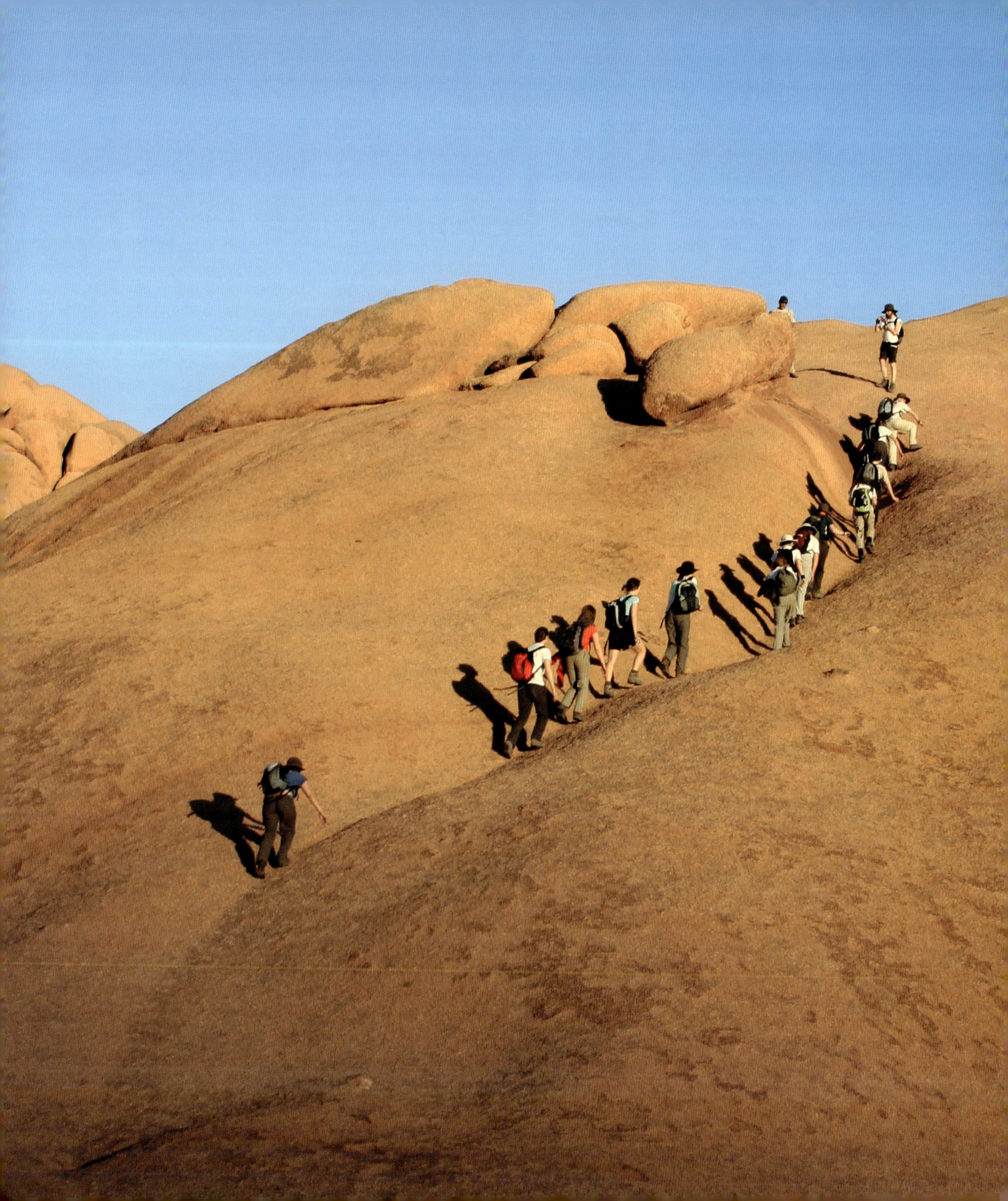

after Sixth Form – as witness the number of ex-Withington girls now undertaking careers across the world.

Withington Girls' School: A celebration of the first hundred years reported that "girls are made increasingly aware of the wider world. They involve themselves in fundraising for many charities; they take part in national and local competitions; they travel at home and abroad". It would have been hard however to predict the extent of the School's current worldwide links.

Increasing understanding

While worldwide links have increased exponentially in recent years, the value of taking lessons out of the classroom and working in the field has always been recognised for certain subjects, geography and biology in particular. The 1970s field trips to the limestone landscape of Malham in Yorkshire were the forerunners of study trips over the last 25 years to a great variety of places, often much further afield.

During the 1980s, the Sixth Form trips organised by staff – to Russia, Romania, Italy, Greece – marked the beginning of Withington girls' travels to explore exotic landscapes, ancient ruins and cathedrals, all while soaking up new cultural experiences. Geographers, ever eager to understand unique landscapes, have over the last decade watched exploding geysers, explored melting glaciers, stood astride the mid-Atlantic ridge and relaxed in geothermally heated pools as they studied the amazing Icelandic landscape on numerous exciting field trips.

Historians visiting Paris have been captivated by the opulence of the Château de Versailles, which as Head of History Jane Maher says, "helps bring a subject, so far removed

My daughter ... has gained an understanding of how to grow and absorb knowledge and use that knowledge to become a more confident young woman, who can go forth into the huge world outside WGS with the ability to contribute to, and maybe even change, her chosen field.

– A PARENT, 2009

Field trips: biologists in 2005; botanists in Styal woods in 1949.

CHAPTER TEN • WITHINGTON AND THE WIDER WORLD

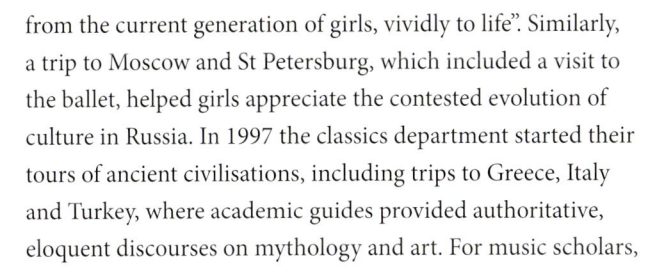

Exploring Russia in 2007 and China in 2012.

from the current generation of girls, vividly to life". Similarly, a trip to Moscow and St Petersburg, which included a visit to the ballet, helped girls appreciate the contested evolution of culture in Russia. In 1997 the classics department started their tours of ancient civilisations, including trips to Greece, Italy and Turkey, where academic guides provided authoritative, eloquent discourses on mythology and art. For music scholars, the Choir Tours to Italy and Barcelona offer the ultimate experience of singing in prestigious venues like the Basilica di San Marco in Venice.

A joint history and politics trip to the USA saw girls explore the more recent history of New York, Washington and other major American cities, even taking in a Broadway show. A history trip to China in 2012 was perhaps the biggest project undertaken. Bustling Beijing with its Summer Palace, Tiananmen Square and the empty Bird's Nest stadium was a once-in-a-lifetime experience for the 30 girls in the group, with other highlights including the Great Wall of China and the Terracotta Army. Soon followed the religious studies trip to Egypt. The party covered 1,500 miles in ten days, including a three-day cruise along the Nile and a trek in the desert, camping out under the stars with Bedouin guides.

I remember reaching the top of Mount Sinai at the end of a trip to Egypt, in time for sunset. We'd been climbing for a few hours in the desert heat and it had been hard going, with lots of moans and groans as well as some real determination on show; some had turned back. Those who reached the summit were pretty ecstatic. One girl turned to her friend and said, "That's the hardest thing I've ever done!" Her friend replied, "Yeah, but it's the best thing I've ever done!" At which point I thought, "I love my job!"

– IAN MCKENNA, THEN HEAD OF RS

All departments find such trips add value to their pupils' learning. They have one special ingredient in common: the chance for pupils to share their teachers' passion for the subject, enabling them to truly connect with the wider world, both present and past, in a way beyond the Founders' initial expectations of their education.

And the experiences are increasingly diverse, with the School ensuring they help girls better understand key events which have changed the course of history. Some Withington Sixth Formers have been privileged to take part in an intensely moving visit to Auschwitz in Poland, an educational programme organised by the Holocaust Educational Trust. The visit allowed time both to feel deep sadness and to be uplifted by the resilience of the survivors. The memories and depth of understanding gained from this experience will stay with these Withington girls forever.

Sporting and cultural exchange

Sporting challenges have also travelled abroad. Lacrosse trips to the USA and, more recently, hockey and netball tours to Australia and South Africa, would have been an impossible dream for the School's Founders, who specified "More prominence will be given to Out-door Games than is usual in Girls' Schools". They would surely have approved of girls competing in true Withington spirit and holding out an important hand of friendship to the teams they met so far from home.

In parallel, the cultural exchange initiatives of the modern languages department have also been highly successful. Since 2007 the Lower Fourths have enjoyed a Parisian Disney theme park extravaganza, while the German department have provided wonderful tours of the German Rhineland and Berlin. The confidence of these younger girls increases as they realise just how much they can understand. The Spanish department tried something a little different, offering joint trips with the food and textile technology department so that girls not only explored historic Spanish towns like Ronda, but also learned about Spanish cuisine from local chefs.

All three modern languages have offered an exchange programme to ensure a deeper cultural experience for the older girls. The French exchange programme was initially set up in the 1990s when Withington was paired with the Lycée St Louis de Gonzague in the heart of Paris. Many girls remember staying with families in their beautiful homes close to the

On tour in South Africa, 2009.

Left: at the Berlin Wall in 2007; above: the Global Student Challenge team in Hong Kong in 2013.

Seine. Current exchange arrangements are with the Lycée des Flandres near Lille, where girls learn about real French culture with their host families while taking part in activities such as sand yachting. To the East, the German exchange was set up in 2007. Here the partner school is the Auguste-Patteberg-Gymnasium, a grammar school in the town of Mosbach in south-west Germany. The Spanish exchange began in 2009, with an all-girls secondary school called La Vall in Ballaterra, north-west of Barcelona. Cultural trips abroad, exploring Gaudi architecture in Barcelona, for example, are matched back home with the delights of Manchester's history and culture, usually featuring Manchester United!

The exchange system introduces girls to a new culture and enhances their language skills, which helps open up more career opportunities later on. Girls are carefully matched according to their personality traits, tastes, likes and dislikes, and, with the advent of social media, many now start communicating on Facebook before meeting. There can be no better way to appreciate a new culture than with someone your own age with a similar outlook, and many girls go on to have lasting bonds with their host families. The girls take the Withington ethos with them, fulfilling the School's aim of creating international friendships.

International competitions allow girls who don't study languages to get to know students all over the world, too. Three AS economics students in particular deserve a special mention, following their success in a Global Student Challenge in 2013. They were invited to Hong Kong to the world semi-finals, after designing a product and business plan. Their product, an innovative portable phone charger, converts kinetic energy from the user's movements into electrical charge. Sonia Patel, Midi Wang and Bethany Jack-Williamson were praised for their teamwork and business flair. In Hong Kong, they met students from 15 different countries, attended lectures on entrepreneurship, and experienced a dynamic, global city. Their visit to Cyberport, a hub of media and technology, gave them a real taste of the new communications that fuse countries across the globe ever closer together.

Making a positive contribution

Over the last decade Withington has looked to organise more trips that make a difference, however small, to the communities

Left: volunteering in The Gambia; above: twins Sheila and Josephine Essendi, sponsored through Kenya's Lugulu Girls' High School by WGS staff.

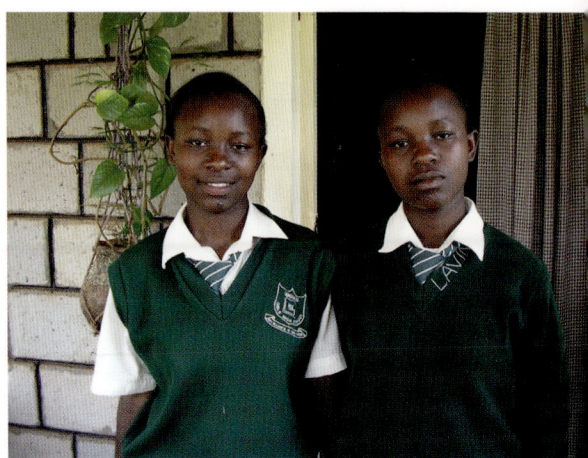

visited. The School has long had a special connection with Africa in particular, as witness its continuing links with Alumna Ann Lipson and her work in Kenya.

The School's connection with The Gambia, West Africa, comes from an initiative by geography teacher Kaeren Browning in 2003. The objective was to create sustainable opportunities for Gambian communities, with education as the focus and helping women the priority. Miss Browning's project manager, Lamin Jammeh, a Gambian taxi driver keen to improve the life of his community, has identified projects that Withington can help progress. Every year a group of highly motivated girls are chosen to raise funds for each project, through initiatives such as car washing, gala dinners and promise auctions. On average £5,000 is raised each year. Girls also travel to The Gambia to undertake work on the ground. Those selected, like all Withington girls, are real team players, hard-working, committed and creative. They paint, teach crafts and games to children, and help women read and write, while assimilating the culture by dancing, eating and singing with local people. Women are often keen to teach the girls new skills in exchange, like tie-dying and speaking Mandinka, the main tribal language of the area.

Now, Withington in The Gambia is a standalone charitable trust, set up by Miss Browning. To date, money raised by the girls has been channelled into work on a series of projects, including two adult literacy centres in rural areas, pedal-driven sewing machines, a nursery school called Mama Tamba, and a farming scheme. All are very appropriate for the rural communities and will be sustained long after the girls have left The Gambia. It is wonderful to think that their special qualities have touched the lives of the Gambian people they meet and will never forget.

Mrs Janet Pickering, Headmistress when the Gambia expedition was first conceived, embraced the huge educational value of Withington's links with Africa. She accompanied teams to The Gambia and Uganda and, after meeting with the Headmistress of Wanyange Girls' School (another WGS!) in Uganda, set about mobilising Withington to help provide equipment the school so desperately needed.

Withington's connections with Africa continue to expand. The year 2014 saw Upper Sixth girls supporting two schemes in Uganda: a special needs nursery being set up by the Small Steps Foundation charity, and a home for 23 boys living on the street set up by the African Street Children Organisation (ASCO) project. The ASCO project itself originated from a group including two WGS girls, Liberty Bridge and Olivia O'Malley, who taught English at Wanyange during their gap years. This is an example of the way work initiated by the School inspires

CHAPTER TEN • WITHINGTON AND THE WIDER WORLD

Ann Lipson

Ann Lipson was a pupil at Withington from 1949 to 1956. After graduating from Manchester University, she taught in England until 1974 and then went out to Kenya to teach physics at Lugulu Girls' High School, on a government programme which sent A-level teachers to Kenyan schools. Ann's original contract was for two and a half years, but she stayed more than 24 years in the same school – long after they discontinued A-levels in Kenya! She retired in 1998 to nearby Kimilili, where she is actively involved with the work of IcFEM (Interchristian Fellowships' Evangelical Mission). Part of this work involves sponsoring needy students through their education, a programme to which WGS staff and pupils have contributed for over 20 years.

Ann has maintained her links with WGS and made many visits to talk to pupils about her work. This has inspired the School community to raise money to support a variety of projects, and establish pen-friend links between Withington and Lugulu girls. In 1995 WGS raised £1,700 towards the cost of a borehole so Lugulu could have clean drinking water, successfully reducing the risk of typhoid. In 2001 the WGS Senior Club arranged a very successful concert at the School featuring Alumna and ENO soloist Christine Rice, raising £1,000 for children with disabilities in need of corrective surgery. Other significant contributions include over £4,000 for a special needs classroom at Sosio Primary School, £1,000 raised by a school talent show in 2007 for a motorbike needed for outreach work, and £1,000 raised in 2011 towards water harvesting in order to fill the below-ground tank at IcFEM Dreamland Education Centre (Primary School). WGS girls, Alumnae, staff and parents are proud of the School's links with Ann and the work of IcFEM and will continue to support their worthwhile work into the future.

Of her time as a pupil at Withington, Ann recalls …

The Main Hall – taking the entrance exam, and three years later being summoned to hear from Miss Bain that the King had died and we now had a young Queen. Years after that, in Kenya, I met the man who had driven her on her sad journey from the Treetops Hotel to Nairobi to fly home to the UK. School plays were big events, then as now. I have vivid memories of doing sound effects in Macbeth. "I go and it is done – the bell invites me" – I was the bell! For my "service to the community", for the Queen's Guide Award, I cleaned the art room equipment every day for about a year, and helped look after the newts in the biology lab. Both good jobs for a quiet, non-sporty type, and I think our year saw a record number of Queen's Guide Awards! My younger sister, Judith, an excellent tennis player and very good all-round sports person, sadly died of leukaemia in 1990. My mother and I gave the tennis cup and trophy cupboard outside the Sports Hall in her memory. Judith was Miss Hulme's first Head Girl, and went on to become a metallurgist.

Bernie O'Neal

pupils to take forward its projects and make a difference themselves.

Girls are involved in foreign expeditions and projects not only to Africa but to all corners of the globe, where they face environments that are challenging in the extreme. World Challenge trips to Bolivia, Namibia, Mongolia, Tanzania and India have involved girls in huge fundraising schemes to achieve the minimum £3,000 for each project. Once there, they are responsible for organising treks across difficult and exacting terrain, and working intensively on community projects. The girls who travelled to Mongolia built two Yurts for homeless people living under stairwells. Highlights for Jane Maher, who accompanies many of the expeditions, include her team reaching the summit of Mount Kilimanjaro, "resulting in hugs, tears and the most joyous feeling", and watching girls learn how to mix concrete by hand to build a playground for children in Namibia

Travel shaping the future

Pupils who take part in overseas projects and expeditions leave school equipped with the ability to travel safely and confidently, and, vitally, a vision of how they want to make their mark on the world. The many girls who independently embark on responsible travel after school attests to the way a Withington education fosters a hunger for exploration and learning that, in turn, creates interest in, rather than fear of, the unknown.

Recognising this value of travel, the Senior Club created a Travel Bursary for Alumnae to aid research or charitable work abroad for girls wishing to take a gap year trip. One of the first recipients, in 2002, was Rachel Green. The bursary helped fund her three-month stay at a clinic in the Ghanaian bush. She reported back, "I weighed babies under the shade of numerous mango trees, took a lot of blood pressures and listened to a lot of foetal heartbeats". Her account conveys the enthusiasm of a first-year medic and the deep privilege she felt at being given a chance to work in this fascinating country. Hannah Buckley, who left in 2005, took a gap year after university, spending her time as a volunteer at an orphanage in Kenya. A small concrete building with a tin roof set in dense green forest became her home for several months. She recognises that her interest in knowledge sharing and relationship building was something Withington inspired, especially her experience as a member of the team that first pioneered the charity mission to The Gambia.

It would seem that ambition to discover new places doesn't end along with gap year travels. Our *Newsletter*s are punctuated with tales of past pupils embarking on careers that take them all over the world. To name a few, Alumnae including Helen Miller and Annadele Bouch joined the Diplomatic Service, with varied overseas postings; Natalie Cohen became a medical

Danielle Morley

Danielle Morley left WGS, where she was "a little bit of a rebel, or I like to think I was", in 1987. At the School from the age of seven to 18, she was one of the few pupils at the time to take a gap year, before studying law at Sheffield University. She practised as a solicitor, but soon realised that fate had something different planned for her. After volunteering in Romania at an orphanage and psychiatric hospital, Danielle completed a Master's degree in global environmental change, and then worked for Water Aid. Later she founded her own independent charity, Freshwater Action Network, working in partnership with Water Aid and with a network of non-governmental organisations which operate globally, influencing water policy and making great efforts to secure safe, clean water and sanitation for those who need it. Their collective work eventually resulted in the Human Right to Water and Sanitation being recognised at the UN; and Danielle frequently represents the voice of NGOs and civil society in global forums. She says it is "very satisfying to know that in some way I'm contributing towards the progression of society".

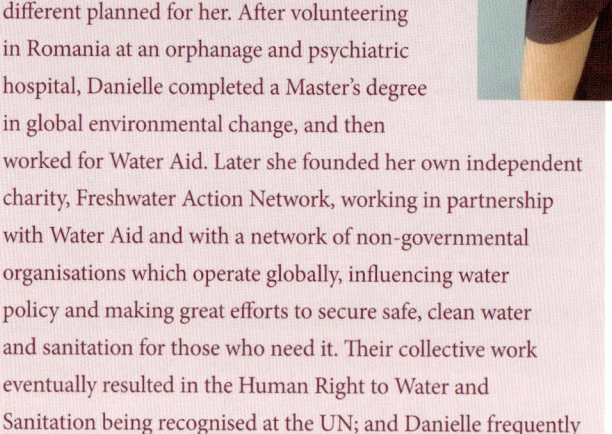

Raeesah Jusab

CHAPTER TEN • WITHINGTON AND THE WIDER WORLD

Elaine Lipworth

Elaine Lipworth, of Withington's class of 1975, is an international journalist living in Santa Monica, California. She is the Hollywood reporter for the *Mail on Sunday*'s *YOU* magazine, and also writes for the *Guardian*, *The Times* and the *Daily Telegraph*. Her work takes her to film sets all over the world, allowing her to rub shoulders with high-profile stars such as Leonardo DiCaprio, George Clooney and Natalie Portman. Elaine remembers Withington with great enthusiasm and affection, saying the School cemented her "lasting love of literature and writing". Highlights include playing Maria in *Twelfth Night*, absolutely loving *The Importance of Being Earnest* and *The Rivals*, and being inspired by teachers Mrs White, Miss Burton (Mrs Hastings) and Miss Boucher. Elaine studied history at London University and post-graduate journalism at the University of Wales, and also has an MA in spiritual psychology from the University of Santa Monica. She worked in radio and TV before focusing on print journalism, earning the International Journalist of the Year Award at the 49th Annual ICG Publicists Awards in LA, in 2012. Withington not only gave Elaine "an amazing group of friends" but also taught her to "express herself, speak her mind and be courageous", qualities which have seen her in good stead in her career.

Elaine's choice of Founders' Day book: a collection of poems by Leonard Cohen.

Alice Gandee

A very fine preparation for being sent out into the world. The feeling of having inherited a good inheritance, of eagerness to go forward to all the wealth of knowledge available. A love of books and of the outdoor world, an interest in other people, the sense of life as a great adventure.

– EVELYNE SCOTT, A PUPIL IN THE 1890S,
LOOKING BACK 60 YEARS LATER

malpractice lawyer in New York; investigative journalist Emma Slater reported on US drone use in Somalia – the Withington ethos of a sense of adventure and determination is ever apparent.

Some girls reconnect with the School and share their experiences at Alumnae careers conventions. Claire Smithson is one of those pupils. After studying medicine at Newcastle University she was posted to Maua hospital in Kenya, and is still there, 24 years later. Claire's work with the hospital's HIV clinic and AIDS orphans in particular touched the Withington community. Now the whole school is involved in biennial fundraising that goes towards shelters, materials for the children and even some blood tests for the clinic. Over the last decade the School's Charity Dance Competition has been a wonderfully inclusive event, with every Form involved in an atmosphere of competitive fun. To thank Withington, Claire sent us a film of the Kenyan children dancing, with happy smiles, as they celebrated moving into their new shelters. Seeing children dance just like they had touched our pupils' hearts. It made them aware that these children, with whom they felt little connection before, are just like them. Showing footage of projects and trips and having guest speakers in assemblies has always been an important way of making girls understand other countries and encouraging them to get involved in future schemes.

Withington girls who take the School's ethos, commitment and vision out into the world inspire the rest of the school community. As globalisation brings once-distant destinations closer, enhancing education and cultural understanding through international travel and work will become an ever more important part of each Withington girl's experience.

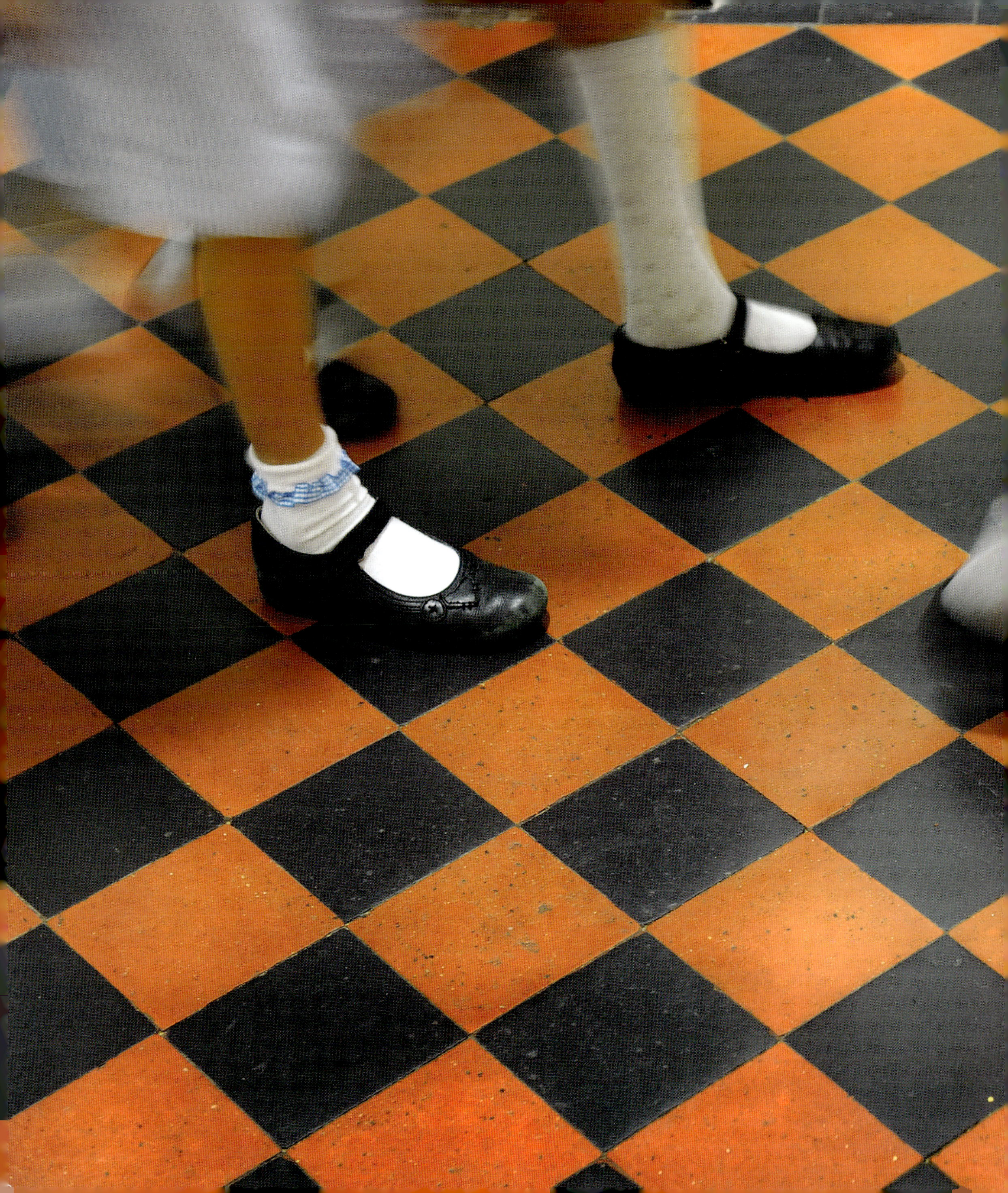

> "On an Anniversary like the present, one of the stepping-stones as it were in the stream of time, we all of us rejoice in looking forward"
>
> – ADOLPHUS WARD, 1911

About the Authors

Jen Baylis is Head of Drama and of the Upper Fifth at Withington. A former WGS pupil, she was Artistic Director of Northern Youth Theatre and has worked on many community and education theatre projects. Her favourite school moments come "when you are working together with a team of staff and students with shared purpose and passion. It is a delight and a privilege."

Julie Buckley is Head of Geography, an Alumna, and a memorable school moment has to be when "at the end of the final Assembly July 1973 to my genuine surprise my name was announced as the newly elected Head Girl. Everyone started stamping their feet on the wooden floors and clapping and I clearly remember a feeling of sheer emotion as I climbed up onto the platform to receive my badge."

Kathryn Burrows is Head of the Junior School, a former Head Girl and a parent. She really enjoyed her time as a pupil, being involved in all aspects of school and playing as much sport as possible: "I never imagined that I would be back at Withington in the same role as Miss Hunter!"

Anthony Burton, museum curator, writer and university lecturer, was an observer of WGS at fairly close quarters because he is the brother of Monica Hastings.

Christine Davies is Head of English, and, amongst other things, oversees the production of *Scrawl*, the school magazine. She and the following Sixth Form *Scrawl* journalists put together the profiles of Withingtonians that you will find throughout this book: **Theodora Critchley, Brittany Fanning, Alice Gandee, Olivia Harman, Raeesah Jusab, Rosie Martland, Julia McCarthy, Ella Pennington, Vidya Ramesh** (*Scrawl* Editor)**, Isabella Risino, Natalie Robinson, Emma Willan, Lauren Woodhead, Natalie Wynn**

Clara Edge teaches English and drama, and is also Head of Personal, Social, Health and Citizenship Education.

Mhairi Ferrol is Head of PE, and of the Lower Fifth. A former Scottish international hockey player, she enjoys all sport and travel and her favourite WGS moments include sports tours to Singapore, Australia, Fiji and South Africa, alongside numerous ski trips to Europe and North America.

Ruth Fildes is Head of Art and has recently completed a Teacher Maker MA course at Manchester Metropolitan University. Her personal work focuses on drawing, printmaking and stop-motion animation, and she exhibits regularly.

Clare Flynn, a former pupil, was Director of Development from 2008 until December 2013, when she joined an international philanthropy management firm. She was also on the editorial committee for this book.

Sarah Haslam is Deputy Head of WGS. She has held this position since 2007, succeeding Dr Mary McDonald onto the Senior Leadership Team. She joined the School to teach English in 1995 and has also been Head of Personal, Social, Health and Citizenship Education, and, as Head of both the Lower and Upper Fifth, was one of the inaugural team of Heads of Year.

Monica Hastings attended WGS from 1954 to 1964 (Head Girl 1963/64), returning as a teacher until 2006 (with a gap for motherhood – her daughters attended WGS). She was involved with the Alumnae association for many years, including two stints as Secretary. Monica's Founders' Day book was *The Concise Cambridge History of English Literature*: "I was off to read English in London. It was very useful then and still is today."

About the Authors

Val Hempstock is a former pupil, teacher (of mathematics), Governor, and expert in the School's history. She left WGS in 1956 and for her Founders' Day presentations chose *The Ascent of Everest* by John Hunt and a text book on University Mathematics.

Lucille Holden, former Head of Classics, continues to teach part-time at the School at present.

Joanna Howling is Head of Classics and an Eco Warriors co-ordinator.

Margaret Kenyon was Headmistress of WGS from 1986 to 2000. A favourite anecdote: "I always hugely enjoyed interviewing the girls who had taken our entrance exam and done well. One ten-year-old, already in the Junior School, when invited to ask me something, paused and then said, 'If it's not a rude question, what do you do all day?' What spirit, I thought. She'll go far."

Anne Kirkham studied art history at Manchester University and is now a research associate there. She is a Governor and Alumna of WGS, and for her Founders' Day presentation chose a picture book on *The Edwardian Season.*

Elisabeth Lee is Chair of the Governing Body. She recently retired from her position as a consultant with the leading law firm Mills & Reeve LLP after a legal career of over 30 years specialising in the insurance industry. She is also a member of the Board of Manchester Metropolitan University and a Patron of the Withington 100 Plus Bursary Appeal. Her daughter Antonia was Deputy Head Girl at Withington in 2000.

Sasha Johnson Manning is a composer, former pupil, and now Governor. For her Founders' Day presentation she chose *Six Suites for Unaccompanied Cello* by Bach and Vivaldi's *Cello Sonatas.*

Sue Marks was appointed Headmistress of WGS in 2010, having held the same position at Tormead School, Guildford since 2001. Her favourite Withington moments are the school assemblies organised by the girls in their form groups, which "give full range to the scope and extent of their wide (and sometimes extraordinary) interests and their amazing talents".

Mary McDonald, a former Deputy Head and Head of Biology, taught at Withington for 35 years, seeing through many Founders' Days!

Ian Mckenna has the distinction of being the first man on the School's Senior Leadership Team. He succeeded Dr Lorraine Earps as Director of Studies in 2013, having previously been Head of the Lower and Upper Fifth and Head of Religious Studies.

Yorke Menzies is Head of French and of the Third Form. A former pupil, she is proud of her contribution to the development of the overseas trips programme, setting up the French exchange link with the Lycée des Flandres and the annual Lower Fourth Disney and La Rochelle trip.

Bernie O'Neal is Head of Learning Support and of Psychology. As WGS's Charity Co-ordinator since 2006 she has been involved with the Kenya projects and has accompanied a number of the trips to The Gambia. "It is a privilege to coordinate the girls' marvellous fundraising efforts and experience first-hand some of the benefits to those in need, both at home and abroad."

Janet Pickering was Headmistress from 2000 to 2010: "Among my numerous favourite Withington moments are being moved to tears of 'uplifted joy' by the girls singing in St Mark's Basilica,

Venice, during the choir tour of 2003 and, every year, being reduced to tears of laughter by their creative wit and ingenuity in the House Play and Carol competitions."

Mary Rawsthorn, a former Head of PE, taught at Withington for 24 years. There were "too many happy moments to choose one. Really, any time a girl learnt to perform a new skill, her satisfaction was mine."

Jessica Richards teaches PE and is now a lacrosse specialist despite knowing very little of the sport when first appointed! She is also Head of Scott House and organises Sports Day.

Jillyan Ross taught at Withington for 29 years. She was Head of Chemistry, Head of Science, and the School's first Director of Studies. A particular interest is bridge, and she founded the School's Bridge Club.

Gilly Sargent has been Director of Music since 2005, and has also run her own performing arts company. She has enjoyed "all the fantastic opportunities afforded by my time at Withington, above all working alongside some truly talented young ladies."

Sharon Senn is the School's first Bursar, a member of the Senior Leadership Team, and Clerk to the Governors and to the WGS Trust. Passionate about music and fitness, she is a regular piano accompanist at Junior School Assemblies and Associated Board exams. Lunchtime fitness classes are "a great opportunity for staff and girls to go through 'the pain barrier' together!"

Cristina Vilela is Head of Chemistry, Oxbridge co-ordinator, former Eco Warriors co-ordinator, and a member of the "Withy Wonders" marathon team.

Jude Wallis is Head of Politics and Deputy Head of the Sixth Form, and along with Sarah Haslam is responsible for the training and running of the Peer Support programme.

Nadine West teaches in the English department and is the School's Debating Co-ordinator and Head of Lejeune House. She also runs a Graphic Novel Club to share her love of literary comics. Nadine is currently studying for an MA in Creative Writing.

Diane Whitehead taught Form I for four years and Lower II for 21 years, and taught English in the Senior School. She was also a tireless organiser of fundraising for Barnardo's.

Above: Vidya Ramesh, editor of Scrawl, *the school magazine; left: members of the* Scrawl *team who contributed to this book.*

ABOUT THE AUTHORS

L to R, top to bottom: contributors to this book in the order in which they appear on pages 146–8.

149

Governance

"The quality of governance is excellent. Governance strongly supports the aims and ethos of the school. All members of the governing body are highly committed to the school. They come from a range of professional backgrounds, and their shared expertise … contributes … to the development of the school." – 2013 Inspectors

It has been ever thus; and we acknowledge here the vital part the School's Governors have played over the years in Withington's evolution, and in ensuring good governance and sound finances.

Chairs of the Governing Body

1890–1891
Professor A.W. Ward LittD LLD
Principal of Owens College; Vice-Chancellor of the Victoria University; Master of Peterhouse College, Cambridge

1891–1932
C.P. Scott Esq. MA LLD
Editor, then owner, of the *Manchester Guardian*

1932–1942
Professor E. Fiddes MA LLD
Ward Professor of American History and Senior Pro-Vice-Chancellor, the University of Manchester

1942–1945
Lady Simon of Wythenshawe MA LLD
Educationalist; Chairman of Manchester Education Committee

1945–1967
R.H.E. Wilkinson Esq. FCA JP
President of the Manchester Society of Chartered Accountants; Lecturer at the University of Manchester

1967–1972
Professor W.I.C. Morris MB ChB MSc FRCS Ed FRCOG
Professor of Obstetrics and Gynaecology, the University of Manchester

1972–1987
Dr V. Knowles OBE MA LLD
Registrar of the University of Manchester

1987–1995
Professor D.S.R. Welland MA PhD
Professor of American Literature and Pro-Vice-Chancellor, the University of Manchester

1995–1997
Sir John Zochonis BA LLD
Philanthropist; Chairman of Paterson Zochonis PLC; Chair of the Council of Manchester University; Deputy Lieutenant and High Sheriff of Greater Manchester

1997–2006
Professor K. Perera BA MA PhD Hon LLD
Chair of Educational Linguistics and Pro-Vice-Chancellor, the University of Manchester

2006–
Mrs E. Lee LLB
Lawyer specialising in the insurance industry; recently retired consultant with Mills & Reeve LLP; member of the Board of Manchester Metropolitan University

Headmistresses of Withington Girls' School

1890–1891
Miss M.S. Ker
Girton College, Cambridge
Mathematics

1891–1896
Miss M.I. Gardiner
Newnham College, Cambridge
Natural Sciences

1896–1901
Miss A.D. Greenwood FRHistS
Somerville Hall, Oxford
History

1901–1908
Miss H.A. Ashworth
Royal Holloway College, London
English

1908–1938
Miss M.A. Grant OBE
St Hugh's College, Oxford
Modern History

1938–1961
Miss M.E. Bain MA
University of Edinburgh
English Language and Literature

1961–1985
Miss M. Hulme BA
Girton College, Cambridge
Mathematics and Moral Sciences

1986–2000
Mrs M. Kenyon DL MA
Somerville College, Oxford
Modern Languages

2000–2010
Mrs J.D. Pickering BSc
University of Sheffield
Biochemistry

2010–
Mrs S.E. Marks MA Adv Cert Ed Man CertTh
Jesus College, Oxford
Philosophy, Politics and Economics

Note: The University of Oxford awarded degrees to women from 1920; the University of Cambridge from 1948

Forms and Years

WGS and National Curriculum Names

Junior School

WGS	National Curriculum
Transition	Year 3
Form I	Year 4
Lower II	Year 5
Upper II	Year 6

Senior School

WGS	National Curriculum
Third Form	Year 7
Lower Fourth	Year 8
Upper Fourth	Year 9
Lower Fifth	Year 10
Upper Fifth	Year 11
Lower Sixth	Year 12
Upper Sixth	Year 13

Most Popular Girls' Names at WGS

An update on the changing fashions in girls' names first charted in *Withington Girls' School: A celebration of the first hundred years.*

	1894	1920	1950	1990	2014
1.	Sarah	Mary	Ann(e)	Sarah	Hannah
2.	Emma	Dorothy	Judith	Catherine	Charlotte
3.	Florence	Margaret	Margaret	Cla(i)re	Sophie
					Eleanor
4.	Victoria	Kathleen	Elizabeth	Emma	Olivia
5.	Helen	Joyce	Susan	Caroline	Isobel
					Natasha
					Ellie
					Sophia
					Emily
					Katie
					Sarah
					Jessica
6.		Marjorie	Barbara	Katie	
7.		Muriel	Christine	Rachel	
8.		Florence	Jennifer	Fiona	
			Hilary		
9.		Ruth	Helen	Laura	
		Betty	Janet		
10.		Mabel	Joan	Helen	
		Helen		Victoria	
		Freda			

Resources

Passim

School Archives
School Website
School *Newsletter*s, 1904 to present
Inspection Reports, 1893 to present
Marjorie Hulme, *History of the School*, 1990
Marie Green, *Withington Girls' School: A celebration of the first hundred years*, 1991
The Withington Hymn Book

Chapters One and Two

Derek Gillard, *Education in England: A Brief History*, at www.educationengland.org.uk
Gillian Avery, *The Best Type of Girl: A History of Girls' Independent Schools*, 1991
Gary S. Messinger, *Manchester in the Victorian Age: The Half-known City*, 1985
J. L. Hammond, *C.P. Scott of the Manchester Guardian*, 1934
The Oxford Dictionary of National Biography

Chapter Three

School *Newsletter*s 1990–2012
Independent Schools Inspectorate Reports of 2007 and 2013

Chapter Six

The Bain Collection:
1 Joyce Hill in *Withington Girls' School: A celebration of the first hundred years*, 1991, p. 29
2 http://www.edinburghmuseums.org.uk/Venues/City-Art-Centre/Collections/Fine-Art/Scottish-Art-Movements/The-Edinburgh-School (accessed 27 August 2013)

Chapter Nine

1 *Manchester Guardian*, 29 July 1911
2 English Indices of Deprivation Report, 2011 (www.gov.uk/consultation/english-indices-of-deprivation)
3 Independent Schools Inspectorate Integrated Inspection Report, 2013 (www.isi.net)
4 *Manchester Guardian*, 29 November 1930

List of Subscribers

This book has been made possible by the generosity of the subscribers listed below.
Those 125 subscribers who responded to the **First to 125** challenge are listed in **bold**.

Ruth Adams	1968–74	Vivien Blundell	
Susan Adams (née Edgar)	1964–71	(née Woodall)	1955–62
Chlöe Adlestone	**2001–12**	**Sophie Bolam**	**2010–**
Libby Adlestone	**2011–**	Lindsay Bouch	1964–74
Tara Adlestone	**2001–11**	Florence Bradshaw	2013–
Angela Adshead	2004–14 (Staff)	Charlotte Bream	2010–
Jane Allen (née Furnival)	1942–8	Imogen Breeze	2013–
Milly Allweis	2012–	**K. Barbara Broadhurst**	
Natasha Anson	2012–	**(née Easton)**	**1940–7**
Lexi Archer	**2011–**	**Amy Jo Brownson**	**2010–**
Melissa Armitt	1997–2004	Helen Buckley	1954–64
Savannah Arora	2014–	**Mildred Burnell**	**1947–54**
Sophia Arora	2010–	Clare Burrell	1971–9
Dita Aswani	1983–90	**K. Burrows**	**1972–8**
Sameeha Atif	2014–	Abigail Bush	2000–9
Ella Baggaley Simpson	2005–12	**Jennifer R. Bushrod**	**1954–63**
Giulia Baggaley Simpson	2007–14	Daisy Eleanor Button	2013–
Charlotte Bailey	**2003–10**	Pauline Cakebread	
Suzanne Bailey	1988–2000	(née James)	1969–76
Lexi Baker	2010–	**Maud F.A. Callery**	**2005–**
Viola Baker	2008–	Lara Calmonson	2013–
Dorothy M. Barker		Cynthia Calvert	
(née Ginger)	1936–43	(née Taylor)	1953–60
Franzi Barnard		Dendy Cannon	
(née Hobson)	**1961–8**	(née Evans)	1948–54
Sophie Bashich	2010–	Judy Cardnell	1963–73
Em Bate	2012–	Imogen Carlson	2006–
Katie Batham	**2012–**	Penny Carter	
Eve Beckford	2012–	(née Wakefield)	1959–69
J. Belford	**1956–66**	**Betty Charlton**	
Kea Ruby Olivia Bell	2009–	**(née Pennington)**	**1940–3**
Sarah Berman	1991–2002	Anisha Chopra	2008–15
Clara Rose Bernstein	2008–15	**Vivien Chung**	**2002–9**
Josie Berry	2010–	**D.M. Claridge**	
Sara Bhatti	2010–	**(née Crowther)**	**1939–45**
L. Pamela Birley	**1940–50**	**Hannah Clark**	**2009–**
Christine Blakeley	1967–77	Laura Clayson	2004–11
Georgie Conlan	2009–	Katie Evans	2013–
Andrea Connell	**1979–86**	Ann Fairman	1951–61
Helen Corlett	**1968–78**	Mhairi Ferrol	2002– (Staff)
Ellena Cotton	**2002–13**	Carolyn Field	
Helen Coubrough	2012– (Staff)	(née Goldstein)	1959–66
Judy Cowan	**1954–64**	Joan Fields	
Terry Cowell	1957–67	(née Richmond)	1958–65 (Staff)
Rosalind Cowie	1990–98	Ruth Fildes	2009– (Staff)
Hazel Cranmer	2010–	Jane Fink	1975–85
Michèle Crawford	1960–7	**Hannah Fitzgerald**	**2005–12**
Laura Cress	**2001–8**	**Laura Fitzgerald**	**2009–**
Wendy Critchley		Clare Flynn	1989–2000, 2008–14
(née Jackson)	1949–56	(Staff)	
S.A. Darbyshire	(Former staff)	Sarah Foot	1972–9
Anisha Das	2011–	**Talia Foster (née Kahn)**	**1988–95**
Sreya Das	2014–	**Dr Jennifer Freeman OBE**	
Antonia Davies	2009–	**(née Watson)**	**1956–63**
Georgina Davies	**1995–2002**	Annabel Fryer	1986–95
Laura Davies	1951–6	**Briony Garety**	
Rebecca Dawson	2012–	**(née Young)**	**1960–7**
Jennifer Deay		Claire Garety	1981–91
(née Patten)	1955–62	**Fiona Gascoigne**	
Judi Dixon (née Cole)	1966–73	**(née Brooks)**	**1967–70**
Madeleine Dodd	2009–	Claire Gascoyne	1987–98
Aileen Doherty	**1962–9**	Natalie Gascoyne	1995–2006
Chantelle-Maya		Pauline Gavan	2002– (Staff)
Dolatshahi-Fard	2007–	Sasha Geim	2007–
Jenni Duffell (née Taylor)	**1992–9**	**Abigail L. Goddard**	**2005–12**
K. Eckersall	2014– (Staff)	**Emily J. Goddard**	**2004–11**
Ellie K.F. Edwards	2007–	Dawn Goldstein	
Bridget Eickhoff	1967–74	(née Salem)	1980–91
Dr Rosemary Ellerby		Nicole Goode	1992–2002
(née Barnes)	**1946–54**	Hannah Gorlizki	2009–
Kathryn Ellis (née James)	1972–9	**Janette Gould**	
Angela English	1955–65	**(née Bailey)**	**1970–7**
Judith English		Margaret Grant	
(née Roberts)	1983–94	(née Carrington)	1944–51

LIST OF SUBSCRIBERS

Leia Rose Griffin	2010–	Momo Ito	2013–
Shamae Emily Griffin	2013–	**In memory of**	
Yvonne Gunn	**1959–65**	Vera Jackson	1946–54
Laura Hale	2010–	**Catherine Jahre-Nilsen**	**1976–88**
Melissa Hale	2008–	Sanaya Jairath	2010–
Alison Hall	1974–82	Vaani Jairath	2012–
Isabel Hall	1974–82	Annie Jefferies	2000–11
Henna Hameed	2010–	Charlotte Jefferies	2011–14
Alex Handforth	1990–7	Ella Jefferies	2000–9
Florence Hannaby-Cummins	2014–	Caroline J. Jenks	
Alicia Harris	**2010–**	(née Barker)	1965–76
Alexandra Hart		**Dr C.M. Jewell**	**1984–95**
(née Taylor)	1990–7	Katrin Jivkova	2013–
Imogen Hart	1979–86	Victoria Johnson	
H.M. Hastings	**1954–64**	(née Morris)	1976–85
Madeleine Haynes	**2006–13**	**Janet E. Jones**	
Gillian Head		(née Polson)	1949–56
(née Wilkinson)	1960–7	**K.M. Jones (née Hutt)**	**1991–8**
Sonia Hearld		Mary Jones (née Furber)	1967–74
(née Hodgkinson)	1964–71	**Penny Jones**	**2008–15**
Barbara Heath		Khadeja Kahn	2009–
(née Clegg)	1935–40	Sejal Karmarkar	2011–
Val Hempstock	**1949–56,**	Jackie Karran (née Clark)	1964–71
	1983–98 (Staff)	Matilda T.S.E. Kelly	2011–
Barbara Heywood		Catriona Kendrick	2007–14
(née Peel)	1943–51	Alison Kenney	1970–7
Lucy Higginbotham	**2012–**	**Holly Kenyon**	**1995–2002**
Kathleen Rose Hill	2000–7	**Margaret Kenyon**	**1924–31**
Ruth Hill	**1953–62**	Margaret Kenyon	
Joan Hilton		1986–2000 (Headmistress)	
(née Rowlands)	1949–56	Amelia Khan	2012–
Annie Hine	2012–	Afshan Khawaja	1987–9
Katie Hine	2013–	**Amira Khurshid Akhtar**	**2003–13**
Dalia Hannah Hodari	2013–	**Anisa Khurshid Akhtar**	**2006–**
Chris Holmes	**(Former staff)**	**Saira Khurshid Akhtar**	**2003–10**
Brontë Horsfield	2012–	Elspeth King	1952–9
Diane Hughes	**1974–81**	**Sarah Kinney**	**2011–**
Eleanor Hughes	2004–	**Tara Kinney**	**2011–**
Martha Hulme	**1977–84**	Vani Kochhar	2000– (Staff)
Diane Hutton	**1968–75**	Ruby Kwartz	2011–
Franka Stefanie Iliffe	2014–	Tamara Kwartz	2009–
Timea Anna Iliffe	2008–	**Hannah Landsman**	**2013–**
David J. Illingworth, in memory		**Beverley Laniado**	**1975–86**
of Joan E.M. Illingworth		**Harriet Laniado**	**1975–86**

Jemima Laniado	**2012–**	**Ruth Morgan**	**1961–8**
Natalie Laniado	**1975–86**	**Devorah Moritz**	**1987–96**
Susan Laniado		**Judith Moritz**	**1987–96**
(née Gledstone)	1954–7	**Rosalind E. Morrill**	
Sylvia Laniado	**1932–44**	(née Gibb)	1969–76
Yvette Laniado	**1932–44**	**Zakeeya Munshi**	**2011–**
Toni Leden (Staff)	2014–	Nadia Myerson	
Elspeth Lee	1985–96	(née Salem)	1990–7
Joanna Lees	2007–14	Sukanya Nanchahal	2014–
Ann Lipson	1949–56	Ruth Neal	1982–2000 (Staff)
The Loftus Family	2005–15	Charlotte Norbury	2009–
Gwendoline Lord	**1965–72**	Amelia O'Hara	2013–
Carol Lowes		Evelyn O'Sullivan	
(née Pritchard)	1950–60	(née Allan)	1985–90
Uschi Lynas		Rosie Oldfield	1987–94
(née Lightfoot)	1966–73	**Emma Othen**	
Dr Sue Madden	**1999– (Staff)**	(née Jewell)	1981–91
Beryl Mallalieu		Alys Owen	2010–14
(née Rushton)	1946–57	Lucy Owen	2010–14
Gina Mann	2004–	**Amie Page**	**2009–**
Gabriella Marfani	**2011–**	Janet E. Parr	
Sue Marks	**(Headmistress)**	(née Young)	1952–63
Katherine Marles	**1964–74**	Catrin Parry	2012–
Judith Marsden	1961–71	Hannah Parry	2012–
Charlotte Marsh	2013–	Francesca Pathak	1998–2005
Joyce Marshall (née Holt)	1930–9	Leona Paykazadi	2012–
Kedrun Laurie Martyn	1964–71	**Kathleen Payne**	
Syeda Zainab Mazhari	2013–	(née Makin)	1967–71
Morag McCaig	1940–6	**Ella Pennington**	**2008–**
Ruby McCaig	1936–9	Natalie Perman	2011–
Julia McCarthy	2007–	Catherine Pickering	1981–8
Sylvia McCarthy	2011–	Eleanor R. Pike	2000–7
Sadie Francesca McGrane	2011–	Lucinda C. Pike	2002–9
Scarlett McKendrick	2010–	Jill Plumbley	
Ian McKenna	2006– (Staff)	(née Tunnicliffe)	1961–8
Phyllis McMellan Sluce	**1953–60**	**Sheila Porter (née Outram)**	
Margaret McNeill	2003–14 (Staff)	**1958–65**	
Merna McVeigh (Current Governor)		Camilla Poulton (née Lakin)	
Yorke Menzies	1975–82	1985–94	
Freya Metcalf	2009–	**Nicola J. Price**	**1965–75**
Elizabeth Miller	1973–9 (Staff)	Dr Helen Pugh (née Booth)	1962–9
Sarah Mishan	**1930–8**	**Evie Raja**	**2014–**
Pat Moneypenny		**Mia Raja**	**2012–**
(née Wild)	1943–8	Rebecca Louise Ramsey	1995–2006

Neethi Rao	2012–	Tina Sharma	1981–92	Adele Taylor	1988–95	Gillian Wild (née Hurst)	1968–75
Rebecca Reed	2007–14	Emma Elizabeth Shaw	1994–2004	Wendy Taylor (née Wilson)		Helen Wiles	
Zoe Reed	2011–	**Rachael Shaw**	**1998–2005**		1943–54	(née Winward)	1962–9
Janice Ridgley (née Todd)	1945–56	Susan R. Sheppard		Tashy Thomason	2008–15	**Emma Willan**	**2009–**
Steph Roberts		(née Mitchell)	1953–60	Heather Thompson		**Annie Williams**	**2011–**
(née Barlow)	**1992–2003**	Eleanor Shipway		(née Hutchins)	1949–57	**Cheryll Williams**	**1966–73**
Catherine Robins	1976–83	(née Willis)	1970–7	**Maureen Thornton**		Eniola Williams	2011–
Natalie Kate Robinson	2008–15	**Gill Sibley (née Spark)**	**1965–75**	**(née Oliver)**	**1952–7**	**Maddy Williams**	**2008–**
Sally Robinson		Sobia Siddiq	2012–	**Sally Tommins**	**1966–73**	**Scarlett Williams**	**2010–**
(née Crompton)	1946–55	Aisha Slater	2014–	Sarah Toulmin		**Jenifer Christine**	
Jamie-Anne Rochford	2009–	Ella Slater	2011–	**(née Taylor)**	**1985–92**	**Williamson**	**1948–58**
Phoebe Rochford	2012–	**Sarah Smith**	**1988–97**	Barbara Trinick		Catherine Wilson	
Eliza Rooney	2006–13	Bhavya Sobti	2009–	(née Burrows)	1951–6	(née Meredith)	1954–62
Kitty Rooney	2006–	Jane Solomon	1976–85	**Anthea Turner**	**1969–71 (Staff)**	Eleanor Wilson	2008–
Ella Luca Rosenblatt	2012–	**Sonia Sondhelm**	**1969–78**	Olivia Tyrrell	2007–14	Francesca Wilson	2006–13
Katherine J.E. Rowland		Alexia Southern	2006–13	**Stephanie Unsworth**	**1998–2005**	Joy Wilson	
1998–2005		Andréa Southern	2011–	Chloe Vell	2009–	(née Benjamin)	1973–83
Kimberley Royle	1997–2004	**Diane Speakman**	**1949–57**	Gabby Ward	2008–15	Wendy Wilson	
Leanne Royle	2000–7	Ellie Spence	2011–	Lucia Ward	2011	(née McDonald)	1961–8
Sue Royle	1981–8	**Victoria Stewart**		K. Warwick		Audrey Winterbottom	1948–53
Helen Ruberry	**1969–76**	**(née Wood)**	**1991–8**	(née Millington)	1984–95	Rhiannon Mary Wood	1995–2002
Shreya Saravana	2010–	Jean Stirling (née Marsh)	1945–56	Mollie Ellen Olivia Watkins	2009–	Lauren Woodhead	2009–
Gillian Sargent	2005– (Staff)	**Debbie Stone**		**Charlotte West**	**1989–96**	**Diana Wooldridge**	**1959–65**
Tamara Searle	2006–14	**(née Carsberg)**	**1972–8**	**Dr Pamela West**		**Eleanor Marie Wright**	**2013–**
Natasha Senior	2007–14	Ellie Mia Stonehouse	2008–15	**(née Walker)**	**1958–69**	Jean Mary Wright	
Charlotte Senn	**2002–13**	Katy Alice Stonehouse	2012–	Katie Wharton	2012–	(née Lambert)	1934–42
Dr and Mrs Shah		**Sally Stuffins**		Lauren Wheeler	2011–	Anna Millie Yaffe	2009–
Zahra Shah	2011–	**(née Whitehead)**	**1991–8**	Sophie Wheeler	2011–		
Zainab Shah	2010–	**Ailie Summerton**	**1970–7**	Diane Whitehead	1964–99 (Staff)		
Zunaira Shah	2013–	Amira Tankel	2009–	**G. Whittick**	**1974–81**		

Index

Bold denotes authorship or featured quotes
Italics indicates captions for illustrations

100 Plus Bursary Appeal, the 47–49, 54, 93

Adams, Ruth 107
Adamson, Dr 11
Amar, Humna **67**
Anne, Princess 41, *46*, 46–7
Anstice, Judy 81
Ashworth, Alice 22, 23, 26
Assembly Hall, the 46

Bailey, Alison 86–8
Bain, Mary Elspeth 18, *27*, 27, 28–30, 34–7, *35*, *36*, 40, 66, 100, 126, 141
Bain Art Collection, the 100, 102
Baker, Kenneth 75
Barlow, Geoffrey **30**, *30*
Barnard (Hobson), Fran **38**, **65**
Barnes, E.W. *131*, 133
Battye, Miriam 121
Baylis, Jen **92–7**
Beale, Dorothea 10
Bergman-Osterberg, Madame 104
Besso, Betty 26–7
Birley, Pamela **31**
Boddy, Stephen 80–1
Boswell, Miss 82
Bouch, Annadele 142
Boucher, Joyce *36*, 40, *41*, 42–3, 73, 76, 92, 94–5, 143
Bowie, Jill 80
Boyd, Tony 80
Bradford, Michael 106
Bradford, Sheila *41*, 106, 124
Brandrick, Miss 38
Bridge, Liberty 140

Bridgewater Hall 18–19, 53, 86
Brown, Ford Madox 16, 17
Browning, Kaeren 140
Buckley, Hannah 142
Buckley, Julie 72, **134–43**
Burrows, Kathryn *7*, **39**, 39, 53, 55, 75
Burton, Anthony **14–27**, **28–41**
Burton, David 103
Burton, Sarah *103*, 103
Buss, Frances Mary 10

Carstensen, Laura 73
Carter, Sasha *109*, 109
Cartledge, Sheena 51
Centenary Year, the 28, 40, 41, 42–3, 44, 46, 50, 68, 86, 92
Chalmers, Judith 84, *85*, *95*, 95
Chalmers, Millie 95
Chalmers, Sandra 84, *85*, *95*, 95
Chapman, Emma *121*, 121
Charlton, Sir Bobby 129
Chatterton, Tim 87
Chicken, Elinor 75–6
Christiansen, Sarah 111
Clucas, Fiona *41*, 108–10
Cohen, Lesley *76*, 76
Cohen, Michelle 76
Cohen, Natalie 142–3
Connell, Diane 101, 103
Connell, Margaret *36*, 48
Cooper, Harriet 103
Corfe, Ivy 31, 35, *36*, 36, 58, 104
Coutts, Margaret 104
Cox, Brian 51, 122, 129
Critchley, Theodora **121**

Davies, Christine **58–69**, **76**, **95**, 121
David Davies Associates 128
Davies, Emily 10
de la Portas, Abby *41*, 49
De Maine, Hilary 39, *41*, 53
Deacon, Jane *41*, 133
Dean, Andrew 87–8
Dodd, Yvonne 52
Drama Studio, the 50, 52
Duke of Edinburgh's Award Scheme, the 123–5, 130

Earps, Lorraine 80
Eco Warriors, the 52, 53
Eickhoff, Bridget *74*, 74
Emily Simon Society, the 48
Essendi, Josephine *140*
Essendi, Sheila *140*

Fanning, Brittany **109**
Farrell, Jillyan *41*, 52, **78**, 79, 80
Ferrol, Mhairi **109**, 111, **112–13**
Fiddes, Edward 25
Fielden, Jean *41*, 82–4
Fildes, Ruth **98–103**
Finney, M.M. *36*, 40
Firth, Laura 49
Fletcher, Sally 111
Flynn, Clare **32–3**, 49
Foerster, Florian 100–2
Ford, Barbara *41*, 85
Founders' Day 8, 16, 18–19, *24*, 28, 42, 44, 47, 50, 53, 61, 65, 68–9, 86
Froebel, Friedrich 16
Frye (McCaig), Ruby **26**

Gandee, Alice **143**
Gardiner, Margaret I. 22
Garrigan, Mr 50
"Gaudeamus" 18–19, 65–6, 82, 95
Gearing, E.M. 31, 37
Ghyll Head 60, 66, 68, 118
Gilbert, Alan 129
Godwin, Anna 75–6
Goldberg, Charlotte 107
Goulty, Michelle *111*, 111
Governing Body, the 8, 17, 24, 25, 28, 32, 34, 37, 52, 62–3, 129
Grant, Margaret A. *14*, 17, 23–5, *24*, 26–7, 36, 58, 104, 126
Grant (Carrington), Margaret 111
Green, Marie 7, 46, 94
Green, Rachel 142
Greenwood, Alice 22
Gymnasium, the 14, 25, 51, 104, 113

Hallé, Charles 21
Hardisty, Miss 30, 31
Harman, Olivia **113**
Harrison, Miss 101
Haslam, Sarah *7*, **44–55**, 75
Hastings (Burton), Monica **14–27**, **28–41**, *41*, **47**, 53, 93–4, 143
Hempstock (Winstanley), Val **17**, **21**, **35**, **36**, *41*
Heneghan, Joan *41*, 81
Herford, Caroline 8, 11, 16, *20*, 20, 24
Herford, Charles Harold **92**
Herford, William Henry 16
Herford House 58, 107
Heyford, May 129

Hill, P. *36*, 40
Holden, Lucille **17**, 124, 130
Holland, Amy 88
Holmes, Chris 86, 88
Holmes, Sarah 89
Horner, David 39
Howling, Joanna **52**
Hughes, Diane **40**
Hulme, Marjorie 7, *37*, 37–40, 42, 44–8, *46*, 54, **70**, *70*, 108, 112, 126, 129, 132, 141
Hunter, Miss *36*, 39
Hytner, Joyce *93*, 93
Hytner, Sir Nicholas 93

Idowu, Karen 107

Jack-Williamson, Bethany 139
Jammeh, Lamin 140
Jivkova, Katrin **68**
Johnson Manning, Sasha 39, 42, **66**, *86*, 86
Jusab, Raeesah **142**

Keatley, Charlotte 84, 96
Kenyon, Margaret 19, **28**, 40–1, *41*, **42–3**, 44, 46, 46–7, 50, 53, 55, 79, 81, 86, 126–7, 128, 129, 133
Ker, Margaret 22
Kilgore, Michele 124
Kinney, Joanne 52
Kirkham, Anne **100**
Kitchener, Mr **14**
Knowles, Vincent 40
Kocialkowski, Kamilla 103

Lady Barn House 6, 11, 16, 20, 21, 39
Leach, Stella 22
Lee of Trafford, Lord 47–8
Lee, Elisabeth **8**, *8*, 54
Lejeune, Caroline 58
Lejeune, Franziska 58

Lejeune, Helen 58
Lejeune, Louisa 8, 11, 16, *20*, 20, 24, 58
Lejeune House 58, 107
Lewis Holland, Imogen 88–9
Lindsay-Dunn, Ruth *41*, 81, 124–5
Lipson, Ann 140, **141**, *141*, 141
Lipson, Judith 141
Lipworth, Elaine *143*, 143
Lloyd, Fiona 52
Lloyd, Sophie **120–1**
Lockett, Mr 81
Longdon, Tori 89
Loveday, Esther 104

MacMillan, James 86
Maher, Jane 120, 136–7, 142
Mamelok, Pat 42
Manchester Grammar School, The 32–3, 122, 129
Manchester University 14, 21, 24, 33, 106, 129, 141
Manning, Christine *41*, 84, 86
Margaret Kenyon Wing, the 50, 86–7
Marett, Julia 22
Marjorie Hulme Arts Centre, the 6, 38, 42, 61, 65, 84–5, 92–3, 128, 130
Marks, Sue **6–7**, *6*, *7*, *46*, **50**, 53–5, 55, **57**, 64, 81, **82**, 88, 89, 97
Martland, Rosie **93**
McCall, Alistair 54
McCardell, Nan 19, *36*, 40, *82*, 82–4, 88
McCarthy, Julia **73**, 107
McDonald, Mary **18–19**, *41*, 46, 52
Mckenna, Ian *7*, **70–81**, **138**
McQueen, Alexander 103
Menzies, Yorke **118**
Mercer, Miss 76
Merica (McCaig), Morag **34**, **63**, 104
Middleton, Catherine 103

Miller, Helen 142
Morgan (Pimlott), Ruth **33**, **62**
Moritz, Judith *49*, 49
Morley, Danielle *142*, 142
Morris, Amy *36*, 40, *41*, **62**
Morton, Sybil 39, *41*

Nance, Claire *111*, 111
Nastase, Ilie 111
Newcombe, John 111
Newson, Charlotte 102

O'Donnell, Helen 47–9
O'Malley, Olivia 140
O'Neal, Bernie 76, **141**
Orme, Kate 112
Ositelu, Catherine 123
Owens, Clare 89
Owens, John 14
Owens College 8, 14, 17, 20, 21, 128

Parent Teachers Association, the 52, 63
Parnell, Denise *112*, 112
Parry, E.A. 11
Patel, Sonia 139
Patelmaster, Sheanna **119–20**
Peer Support 60–1, 118
Penney, Dr 52
Pennington, Ella **86**
Perera, Katharine 52, 129
Pestalozzi, Johann Heinrich 16
Pickering, Janet 18, **44**, *46*, 47, 50–5, *54*, 63, 72, 93, 96, 111, 113, **125**, 125, **126–33**, *130*, 140
Pickering, Ron 53
Power, Tara **65**
Prouse, Miss 30

Ramesh, Vidya **49**
Rantzen, Esther *19*, 53
Rattle, Sir Simon 89
Rawsthorn, Marjorie *36*, 40, 42
Rawsthorn, Mary **104–11**, 112

Redpath, Anne 100
Renold, Jasmine 81
Rice, Christine 84–5, *85*, 141
Richards, Jessica *107*, 112
Risino, Isabella **103**
Robinson, Elizabeth 76
Robinson, Natalie **128**
Rogoyska, Marta 42
Ross, Jillyan (*see* Farrell, Jillyan)
Rothwell, Dame Nancy 51, 129
Rutherford, Sarah 128

Sargent, Gilly **82–90**, 113
Scott, Charles Prestwich 8, 11, *16*, 16–17, *17*, 22, 24–5, 27, 69, 128–9
Scott, Evelyne **23**, *143*
Scott, Madeline *16*, 16, *17*, 17
Scott, Rachel 8, 11, 17, 22
Scott House 58, 107
Senior Club, the 24, 27, 42, 53, 141, 142 (*see also* Withington Onwards)
Senn, Sharon **7**, **48**, 54
Sharples, Mr *101*, 101
Simon, Dorothea 27
Simon, Emily 8, 11, 16, *20*, 20–3, 25, 27, 28, 104
Simon, Henry 8, 11, 16, *20*, 20–2, 25, 27, 28
Simon, Shena (Lady Simon of Wythenshawe) 21, 25, 28
Simon House 58, 107
Sixth Form Centre, the 48, 52
Slater, Emma 143
Smithson, Claire 143
Sports Day 60–1, 107, 130
Sports Hall, the 19, 46–7, 50, 104, 108, 128
Spurgin, Marjorie 47
Stansfeld, Miss *14*, 104
Steinhal, Theodora 104
Stevenson, Clive 51
Stolle, Fred 111

INDEX

Taylor, Terry 107
Thomas Worthington Design 128
Thompson, Becca 87
Thornton, Suzannah 111

Vell, Chloe *113*, 113
Verity, Emily 31, *36*, 36
Vilela, Cristina **52**

Wallis, Jude **60**
Wang, Midi 139

Ward, Adelaide 16, 133
Ward, Adolphus William 8, 11, **13**, 16, *20*, 20, 128–9, 133, **134**, 145
Waterhouse, Alfred 14
Welland, Professor 42, 47
West, Nadine **116–25**, 130
WGS Trust, the 6, 44, 47, 48, 132
Wheeler, Francisca 129
White, Mrs 143
Whitehead, Diane **21**, *41*

Whittle, Stephen *128*, 128
Whitworth Hall 18–19, 28
Whyte, Flora 107
Willan, Emma **85**
Williams, Mrs 39
Williams, Peggy 129
Wilson (Meredith), Catherine **19**, 35, 36
Withington Onwards 49, 68, *69*
Wollenberg, Susan 89
Wolstenholme, Anna 86

Wood, Erica 42
Woodhead, Lauren **112**
Wooldridge (Hall), Diana **101**
Wynn, Natalie **74**

Yates (Widmer), Anna **31**
Young, Baroness 50

Zochonis, Sir John *50*, 50

Acknowledgements and Thanks

The cover photograph and most of the contemporary photographs in this book were taken by Howard Walker. The majority of historical material comes from the School's archives.

We would like to thank everyone who has helped make this book possible: Hannah Brown, Clare Flynn, Val Hempstock, Amira Khurshid Akhtar, Penny Knipe, Toni Leden and Penny Willis for their hard work and research; Mark Morris for his photography; Angela Adshead and Ann Easton for their support. Our thanks go too to Eliott Peterken of ie-creative for his help with sourcing images and permission to reproduce his own artwork; and to Ruth Lindsay-Dunn, Jane Maher and all staff, pupils and Alumnae whose pictures of school life and travels and other artwork appear in these pages. We are grateful to Marjorie Hulme, Margaret Kenyon and Janet Pickering for their advice and for reviewing material at various stages.

We would also like to thank those listed below for providing or allowing images to be reproduced on the following pages: P 16, birds' eye view of Manchester: Look and Learn; P 17, painting of Madeline Scott: Manchester City Art Gallery; P 28, poster: © The National Archives; P 31, clothing ration book: Mary Evans; P 49, Judith Moritz: Nick Garnett; P 50, Sir John Zochonis: the Zochonis Charitable Trust; P 73, Laura Carstensen: the Equality and Human Rights Commission; P 76, Lesley Cohen: Meilin Sancho; P 74, Bridget Eickhoff: © Institution of Mechanical Engineers; P 85, Christine Rice: Rob Moore; P 86, Sasha Johnson Manning: Naxos/Sally-Anne Heaford; P 93, Joyce Hytner: Act IV; P 100, the Bain Collection and P 128, Stephen Whittle: Sandra Dalton; P 103, Sarah Burton: courtesy of Alexander McQueen; P 104 and 111, badges: Margaret Grant (Carrington) (1951); P 112, Denise Parnell: AELTC; P 113, Chloe Vell: Rui Pedro Godinho; P 121, Emma Chapman: Claire Weir; P 142, Danielle Morley: Isabella Montgomery; P 143, Elaine Lipworth: Getty Images.

Endpapers:
Inside the front cover: aerial view of the School in 1928
Inside the back cover: aerial view of the School in 2008

Towards the Light: A Portrait of Withington Girls' School

2014 © Withington Girls' School and Third Millennium Publishing Limited

First published in 2014 by Third Millennium Publishing Limited,
a subsidiary of Third Millennium Information Limited.

2–5 Benjamin Street, London EC1M 5QL, United Kingdom
www.tmiltd.com

ISBN: 978 1 908990 22 8

All rights reserved. No part of this publication may be reproduced or transmitted in any form or by any means, electronic or mechanical, including photocopying, recording, or any storage or retrieval system, without permission in writing from the copyright owner concerned.

British Library Cataloguing in Publication Data
A CIP catalogue record for this book is available from the British Library.

Project edited by Deborah Coleman
Designed by Susan Pugsley
Production by Debbie Wayment
Reprographics by Studio Fasoli, Verona, Italy
Printed by 1010 International Limited, China